THE LANGUAGE OF WORDSWORTH AND COLERIDGE

General Editor: N. F. Blake

Professor of English Language and Linguistics
University of Sheffield

00076142

THE LANGUAGE OF LITERATURE
General Editor: N. F. Blake

Published titles
The Language of Shakespeare   N. F. Blake
The Language of Chaucer   David Burnley
The Language of Wordsworth and Coleridge   Frances Austin
The Language of Irish Literature   Loreto Todd

Further titles are in preparation

Other books by Frances Austin
The Letters of William Home Clift
Robert Clift of Bodmin Able Seaman

THE LANGUAGE OF WORDSWORTH AND COLERIDGE

FRANCES AUSTIN

STRODE'S COLLEGE
LIBRARY

MACMILLAN

© Frances Austin 1989

All rights reserved. No reproduction, copy or transmission
of this publication may be made without written permission.

No paragraph of this publication may be reproduced, copied
or transmitted save with written permission or in accordance
with the provisions of the Copyright Act 1956 (as amended),
or under the terms of any licence permitting limited copying
issued by the Copyright Licensing Agency, 33–4 Alfred Place,
London WC1E 7DP.

Any person who does any unauthorised act in relation to
this publication may be liable to criminal prosecution and
civil claims for damages.

First published 1989

Published by
MACMILLAN EDUCATION LTD
Houndmills, Basingstoke, Hampshire RG21 2XS
and London
Companies and representatives
throughout the world

Printed in the People's Republic of China

British Library Cataloguing in Publication Data

Austin, Frances
The language of Wordsworth and Coleridge.
—(The Language of literature).
1. Poetry in English. Coleridge, Samuel
Taylor & Wordsworth, William, 1770–1850 —
Critical studies
I. Title   II. Series
821'.7'09

ISBN 0–333–43272–X
ISBN 0–333–43273–8 Pbk

Contents

Prefatory Note   vii

Acknowledgements   ix

Grammatical Terminology   x

Texts and Abbreviations   xiii

1 Introduction   1

2 Experimental Narrative Ballads   15

3 Poems in Ballad Measure   47

4 Blank Verse – Diction   64

5 Blank Verse – Syntax   93

6 Coleridge   122

7 Analysis of Passages   169

8 Conclusion   180

Notes   187

Select Bibliography and Further Reading   195

Index 1 Textual References   199

Index 2 Literary References   201

Index 3 Language Topics   202

To my Mother and Father

Prefatory Note

Both Wordsworth and Coleridge wrote poems for *Lyrical Ballads* (1798) and their names have understandably been linked ever since. They do, indeed, have many things in common, not least their reaction against eighteenth-century modes of writing poetry. Yet there are differences, too, and these determine the pattern of such a book as this. In themselves the contrasts between their poems are enlightening and help us to understand each poet better. But the difficulty is obvious from the start. *Lyrical Ballads* (1798) contains only four poems by Coleridge, whilst Wordsworth wrote the remaining nineteen. The collection opens with Coleridge's *Ancient Mariner* and many books have been written about that poem alone. Nevertheless, if we look at the collected poems of the two writers it is clear that Wordsworth wrote a great deal of first-class poetry and that Coleridge's first-class poetry consists of no more than about twenty pieces. Two of them (*Kubla Khan* and *Christabel*) are unfinished, and some would say that, magical and unique as they are, they never could have been finished. Any book about the two poets together consequently has to reflect in treatment and proportions this almost physical discrepancy in output. However, it would be wrong to judge the merit of the poems by the number of pages given to them. The quality of Coleridge's best poems is very high. This book is not a competition between the two poets but a recognition of their likenesses in some matters and their even greater and quite individual excellences – and sometimes weaknesses – in others. That Wordsworth is given more space and Coleridge less lies in the nature of their respective output of poetry. It does not mean that Wordsworth is being rated above Coleridge.

East Stour, Dorset   FRANCES AUSTIN
September 1987

Acknowledgements

This book could not have been written without the help of many friends and institutions. I am particularly grateful to the librarians of the University of Southampton and the county libraries at Ringwood and especially Sherborne for dealing patiently with requests for books and articles, and to the staff of the Inter Library Loan Service.

I should like to thank the students who contributed to seminars on Wordsworth and Coleridge, and especially the 'matures' at Bishop Grosseteste, Lincoln (1969), who roused my enthusiasm for *The Ancyent Marinere*, and the Shaftesbury Group (1986) for their encouragement.

It is a great pleasure to acknowledge the help I have received from my former student, Valerie Milling, who has responded so promptly to enquiries about certain books not readily accessible. Dr Bernard Jones has given much time to reading my various drafts and has made many helpful suggestions. Above all, Professor Norman Blake has been tireless in answering questions and generous with encouragement, and not only during the writing of this book. I need hardly say that these people are not responsible for the shortcomings that are inevitable in a short book on so vast a subject.

Grammatical Terminology

Inevitably in a book of this kind grammatical terms must be used. Since many readers may be unfamiliar with even 'traditional' terminology and others may be used to different terms used in the various current grammatical 'models', a few words on the usage here will not come amiss.

The basic terms for the 'parts of speech' – noun, verb, adjective, etc. – have been retained as is the practice of most current models of grammar. For explaining and describing the basic structure of sentences Systemic Grammar has generally been followed, sometimes in a modified form. In Systemic Grammar the clause is divided into four main elements: Subject, Verb, Complement and Adjunct. These are represented by the notation S V C A. Subjects and Complements (the term Complement includes both the Object and Complement of 'traditional' grammar) are often 'realised' by nominal groups. A nominal group is a group of words based round a noun which is called the 'head' of that group. An example is 'the swift flowing river with its swirling eddies', where the 'head' is the word *river*. All nominal groups can be used as the Subject of a sentence. Complements are also 'realised' by adjectives or adjectival phrases when they follow the verb *to be* or other 'copula' verbs such as *seem*. Examples are 'the river is *deep*', 'the lion looked *very fierce*'. Verbs are 'realised' by verbal groups. These may consist of a single verb or a verb preceded by one or more auxiliary verbs. 'John *swam* a hundred yards' is an example of the first kind and 'John *would have been swimming* today but he has a cold' of the second. Note that the verb which conveys the 'main' information (called a 'lexically full' verb) comes last in the group. An Adjunct is essentially anything which does not come under one of the other three headings. There are, therefore, various kinds of Adjuncts, but the basic one and that to which the notation A refers in this book is an adverb or adverbial group. Examples are 'merrily'; 'with great courage'; and 'beside the stream' in sentences such as 'he sang *merrily*'; 'he fought the lion *with great courage*'; and 'she knelt *beside the stream*'.

It is now customary in Systemic Grammar to discard the term 'sentence' and substitute 'clause complex'. Readers will find both terms used in this book. 'Sentence' seems too useful a term to be rejected completely but at times 'clause complex' is clearer and more precise because it indicates the clause structure of which the sentence is composed and the way in which those clauses are put together.

The term 'expansion' is a technical term. It is normally used to refer to methods of extending the clause (see M. A. K. Halliday, *An Introduction to Functional Grammar*, Edward Arnold, 1985, pp. 202–16) but here mostly refers to expansion of the nominal group.

One further technical term that may be unfamiliar has been used. This is 'interpersonal', again a term modified from Halliday (see *IFG*, pp. 332–4). It is used for comments of the poet/narrator expressing a personal opinion that occur in the text but are really external to it. Examples are 'I think'; 'it seems'; 'perhaps'; and so on.

Students will find that in most books based on Systemic Grammar the Verbal element is marked with a P for Predicator. As V seems more accessible to those unfamiliar with this grammar it has been adopted here. It is used in J. F. Wallwork, *Language and Linguistics* (Heinemann, 1969). Readers may consult Chapter 5 of this book for a quick guide to the structure of the four main elements of the clause. A fuller exposition of Systemic Grammar will be found in Dennis Freeborn's, *A Course Book in English Grammar* (Macmillan, 1987). Halliday's *An Introduction to Functional Grammar* (see above) is a much more advanced account of Systemic Grammar written by its leading exponent and it is referred to frequently in the notes. It is of particular use for textual studies and may be of interest to those who wish to pursue the subject further. A very useful introductory book on grammar, that shows the relation of traditional grammar to Systemic Grammar, is N. F. Blake,

Traditional English Grammar and Beyond (Macmillan, 1988). For other explanations of a rather more traditional, although up-to-date, kind, the grammars of Randolph Quirk and his collaborators cannot be ignored. The latest of these is R. Quirk *et al.*, *A Comprehensive Grammar of the English Language* (Longman, 1986). An earlier, somewhat shorter version is R. Quirk *et al.*, *A Grammar of Contemporary English* (Longman, 1972), and a simpler version based on this is R. Quirk and S. Greenbaum, *A University Grammar of English* (Longman, 1973).

Texts and Abbreviations

All poems of Wordsworth and Coleridge taken from *Lyrical Ballads* are quoted from *Lyrical Ballads*, eds R. L. Brett and A. R. Jones (London: Methuen, 1963, rev. 1965) (*LB*). Wordsworth's successive versions of 'The Ruined Cottage' are taken from *The Ruined Cottage and The Pedlar*, ed. James Butler (Ithaca, N.Y.: Cornell U.P.; Sussex: Harvester Press, 1979). References to the origins of 'The Female Vagrant' are based on *The Salisbury Plain Poems of William Wordsworth*, ed. Stephen Gill (Ithaca, N.Y.: Cornell U.P.; Sussex: Harvester Press, 1975). Other poems by Wordsworth are quoted from *Poetical Works*, eds Ernest de Selincourt and Helen Darbishire, 5 vols (Oxford: Clarendon Press, 1940–9) and the 1805 text of *The Prelude*, eds Ernest de Selincourt, 2nd edn. rev. Helen Darbishire (Oxford: Clarendon Press, 1959); also available in Oxford Standard Authors, 1960. The 1800 and 1802 Prefaces to *Lyrical Ballads* and the 1800 Note to 'The Thorn' are taken from Brett and Jones's edition of *Lyrical Ballads*. These may also be found in W. J. B. Owen, ed., *Wordsworth's Literary Criticism* (London: Routledge & Kegan Paul, 1974), and the 1800 Preface in Vol. I of *Prose Works*, eds W. J. B. Owen and Jane Worthington Smyser, 3 vols. (Oxford: Clarendon Press, 1974) pp. 118–58. The 1815 Preface to Wordsworth's *Poems* is taken from Vol. III of *Prose Works*, pp. 25–39, abbreviated to *PW*. Wordsworth's letters are quoted from the seven volume edition of Chester L. Shaver, Mary Moorman and Alan G. Hill, which divides into The Early Years (*EY*), The Middle Years (*MY*) and The Later Years (*LY*) (Oxford: Clarendon Press, 1967–88). This edition is a revision of Ernest de Selincourt's six volume edition (Oxford: Clarendon Press, 1935–8). References to letters are followed by the equivalent volume (where relevant) and page number in de Selincourt's edition. Poems of Coleridge, other than those printed in *Lyrical Ballads*, are quoted from *The Poetical Works of Samuel Taylor Coleridge*, ed. Ernest Hartley Coleridge (1975, 1st edn. 1912). Quotations from *Biographia Literaria* (*BL*) are from the Everyman edition (London: Dent 1906, rev. George Watson 1965), to which page references are given. Coleridge's letters are quoted from *Collected Letters of Samuel Taylor Coleridge*, ed. E. L. Griggs, 6 vols. (Oxford: Clarendon Press, 1956–71).

Datings for Wordsworth's poems are mainly based on Mark L. Reed, *The Chronology of the Early Years 1770–1799* (*CEY*) (Cambridge, Mass.: Harvard U.P., 1967) and *The Chronology of the Middle Years 1800–1815* (*CMY*) (Cambridge, Mass.: Harvard U.P., 1975).

M. A. K. Halliday, *An Introduction to Functional Grammar* (London: Edward Arnold, 1985) is abbreviated to *IFG*.

1 Introduction

Although they almost certainly met at Bristol in the summer of 1795, the close friendship between Wordsworth and Coleridge began in the summer of 1797 when Coleridge 'leaped over a gate and bounded across a pathless field' to Racedown (*LY*, IV, 719 [III, 1263]),[1] the house in Dorset where Wordsworth was living with his sister Dorothy. By this time Wordsworth's youthful adventures in France were well behind him. His involvement with the French Revolution had been complicated by his liaison with Annette Vallon, who became an ardent royalist. When his uncles stopped sending him money he was forced to leave France, leave Annette and his baby daughter, Caroline, and return to England. His disillusionment, first when England failed to support the revolution and then when he realised the full horrors of the atrocities committed by it, pushed him to the verge of mental breakdown. A legacy of £900 from his friend Raisley Calvert allowed him to rejoin Dorothy and regain some peace of mind in the tranquillity of the West Country. Coleridge, too, had virtually finished with his dreams of setting up a democratic republic on the shores of the Susquehanna with a group of friends, including his future brother-in-law, Robert Southey. This project they called Pantisocracy. Unwisely, and finally it seems against his will, Coleridge had been persuaded into marrying Sara Fricker and in 1797 they were settled with their first child, David Hartley, at Nether Stowey in Somerset. Coleridge was a published poet and Wordsworth, encouraged by Dorothy, had decided finally to devote all his energies to composition. Both men, therefore, had done with the earlier follies of their post-student days and were open to new experiences. Perhaps this was why their friendship flourished so rapidly.

1

The early years of Wordsworth (1770–1850) and Coleridge (1772–1834) had been both similar and dissimilar. They were orphaned early. Wordsworth's father died in 1783 when he was thirteen and Coleridge's father in 1781 when he was only nine. Wordsworth had also lost his mother before this second catastrophe overtook him. Thereafter their lives followed different paths. Wordsworth remained at his school in Hawkshead and in many ways his life continued unchanged. In 1782, the year following his father's death, Coleridge, however, was packed off to Christ's Hospital in London, where he was desperately unhappy. He did not even return to his native Devon for holidays and remembered the haunts of his early childhood with homesick longing. It was at Christ's, however, that he met his lifelong friend, Charles Lamb.

We are apt to think of both Wordsworth and Coleridge as nineteenth-century poets, which indeed they are. But we tend to forget that their formative years were lived wholly in the eighteenth century. Wordsworth was thirty in 1800 and Coleridge was just two years younger. It is generally held that by the age of thirty a person's linguistic habits are more or less fixed and change relatively little after that. Both men, therefore, had acquired the foundations of their language during the eighteenth century and their early attempts at poetry are firmly in the eighteenth-century tradition. Yet, just before he reached the age of thirty Wordsworth set about one of the greatest linguistic experiments ever undertaken by an English poet. He altered his normal mode of usage and in *Lyrical Ballads*, the joint venture that he began with Coleridge not long after that meeting in 1797, he used a language that was virtually new both to him and in poetry. This deliberate change was to affect all his writing from that time on. Later, in *Biographia Literaria* (1817) Coleridge was to criticise Wordsworth for going too far in the direction of what was considered unpoetic and commonplace, but by then Wordsworth had changed the course of English poetic language. Even Coleridge's poetry written after 1798 cannot be confused with that of his earlier period.

The influence that each poet had on the other has been much discussed and written about. The immediate impression is that Wordsworth's was the greater influence. Certainly, his treatment of Coleridge over *Lyrical Ballads* was somewhat high-handed to say the least. Coleridge appears to have been the less dominant of the two, lavishing uncritical adulation on Wordsworth until the break in their friendship in 1810. This view, however, has been contested.[2] It is also worth bearing in mind that in 'The Eolian Harp' Coleridge expresses the essential attitude towards life and nature that Wordsworth was later to elaborate so fully in *The Prelude* and which is seen in many of his poems in *Lyrical Ballads*. 'The Eolian Harp' was written in the summer of 1795 before either poet had had any influence on the other. Indeed, Coleridge developed a manner of writing blank verse in his 'conversation' poems which was quite unlike anything written in this form before and which almost certainly influenced the blank verse that Wordsworth wrote after his early play in the form, *The Borderers* (1795–6). The relationship between the two men is so complicated, not only by events and writings at the time but by their later recollections, that it is now virtually impossible to disentangle. Another complicating factor is the part played by Dorothy, who was undoubtedly a great influence on both poets. It must also be remembered that they were both influenced by new attitudes that were emerging amongst their contemporaries and in the elder generation among such men as Godwin. Reaction to earlier eighteenth-century ideas was widespread and they were not as completely original in their own thinking as is sometimes imagined. What is certain is that they stimulated and encouraged each other to the extent that much of the best-known poetry of each was the product of the years of their close friendship.

First, however, if we are to understand their use of language, we must look briefly at the literary tradition which Wordsworth and Coleridge inherited. Language cannot be separated from subject and the subject matter of this tradition is therefore important. Two things were central to eighteenth-century poetry: Nature and Man.

The tradition of nature poetry had continued from earliest times, through Spenser, Shakespeare and Milton to the early eighteenth century, and attitudes towards it had changed relatively little. On the whole it was viewed through the classical and pastoral tradition and was generally presented in what seems today an idealised and artificial light. With the eighteenth century, however, nature and the natural landscape began to be described more realistically. Often the two attitudes, the idealised and the realistic, continued side by side and sometimes even merged in one poem. In the earliest poetry of the century, nevertheless, it was of a landscape that had been 'tamed' by man that the poets wrote. This is clear in Pope's early poem *Windsor-Forest* (1704).[3]

> Succeeding monarchs heard the subjects' cries,
> Nor saw displeas'd the peaceful cottage rise.
> Then gath'ring flocks on unknown mountains fed,
> O'er sandy wilds were yellow harvests spread,
> The forests wonder'd at th'unusual grain . . .   (85–9)

Pope's observation of natural phenomena is as sharp as that of Wordsworth or Coleridge but the reader is always aware of the presence of man and human activities:

> With slaught'ring guns th'unwearied fowler roves,
> When frosts have whiten'd all the naked groves;
> Where doves in flocks the leafless trees o'ershade,
> And lonely woodcocks haunt the wat'ry glade.
> He lifts the tube, and levels with his eye;
> Straight a short thunder breaks the frozen sky:
> Oft, as in airy rings they skim the heath,
> The clam'rous lapwings feel the leaden death.   (125–32)

Another view of nature, however, develops quite early in the century. This is nature wild and untamed. It was established well before the middle of the century and became at times excessive and even violent in expression. Two short extracts will demonstrate this kind of poetry. The first is part of 'Winter' from Thomson's *The Seasons* and shows the elemental expression into which this attitude often moved:

> Then issues forth the Storm, with loud Control,
> And the thin Fabrick of the pillar'd Air
> O'erturns at once. Prone on th'uncertain Main,
> Descends th'Etherial Force, and plows its Waves,
> With dreadful Rift: from the mid-Deep, appears,
> Surge after Surge, the rising, wat'ry, War.

Whitening, the angry Billows rowl immense,
And roar their Terrors. . . .   (161–8)

This was published as early as 1726. A description of a tempest
much more acceptable to us today comes in Cowper's *The Task*,
written in 1785, well on into the lifetime of Wordsworth and
Coleridge:

> Mighty winds
> That sweep the skirt of some far-spreading wood
> Of ancient growth, make music not unlike
> The dash of ocean on his winding shore,
> And lull the spirit while they fill the mind,
> Unnumber'd branches waving in the blast,
> And all their leaves fast flutt'ring, all at once.   (I, 183–9)

Something of the effect the elements can have on man's
sensibility appears in these lines and this was, of course, typical
of the later part of the century, as the age of 'feeling' took over
from the age of 'reason'.

After the middle of the century there is a surprising dearth
of well-known names on the poetic scene. Of those that do
occur, Goldsmith, Cowper and, considerably later, Crabbe, were
already beginning to show a shift in the focus of their subject
matter that to some extent prefigures the line Wordsworth was
to take. The impact of Burns came from an independent
tradition. All indicate some interest in the effect nature has on
man and his conduct or emotional responses, although in very
different ways. Crabbe painted a far more pessimistic picture
of village life than Goldsmith had done some thirteen years
before. Goldsmith, lamenting the exodus from the countryside,
idealised, although in a more realistic manner than his predecessors, the rural way of life. Generally, however, emotions
were written about in a rather stilted way, almost as if their
names were verbal counters. To us the writers seem to name
the emotion without attempting to recreate it. Thus emotions
usually appear as personifications. Indeed, Collins in his ode
'The Passions', written about 1746, treats them in just this way.
Any subtle or flexible attitude to the way in which people
respond to external forces was outside the range of mid-
eighteenth-century thinking.

Man and man's place in the universe were an ever present concern of eighteenth-century writers, as of thinkers at all times. We have seen that even in Pope's 'nature' poetry man is never far away. But for the most part poets of the first half of the century, including Pope, were concerned with the man in society rather than in the countryside and, moreover, only with the higher and more educated classes of society, who lived in an urban environment. From his imitations of Horace, which are concerned with human behaviour, to his witty, light-hearted satire, *The Rape of the Lock*, Pope depicts life in fashionable circles. Before Goldsmith and Crabbe there was little written about the ordinary humble citizen or the country dweller. Poets were concerned with morals and human conduct. Necessarily, this led to much verse of a satirical nature, which again addressed itself in the main to the higher ranks of society.

A further development during the eighteenth century was an attraction to the 'horrid' or 'Gothick'. This, too, appears surprisingly early in poetry, although we frequently associate it more with novels of the second half of the century, such as Horace Walpole's *The Castle of Otranto* written in 1764–5, and the works of Ann Radcliffe, whose first novel appeared in 1789. An early poetic example comes in Thomas Parnell's 'A Night-Piece on Death', which was not published until Pope edited a selection of Parnell's poems in 1722. The poet himself died in 1718. The following extract is less 'decorated' than many later writings on such themes:

> Now from yon black and fun'ral Yew,
> That bathes the Charnel House with Dew,
> Methinks I hear a *Voice* begin;
> (Ye Ravens, cease your croaking Din,
> Ye tolling Clocks, no Time resound
> O'er the long Lake and midnight Ground)
> It sends a Peal of hollow Groans,
> Thus speaking from among the Bones.   (53–60)

A later example of the Gothick occurs in 1743 in Robert Blair's blank-verse poem 'The Grave', the very title of which suggests the morbid:

Rous'd from their Slumbers
In grim Array the grizly Spectres rise,
Grim horrible, and obstinately sullen
Pass and repass, hush'd at the Foot of Night.
Again! the Screech-Owl shrieks: Ungracious Sound!
I'll hear no more, it makes one's Blood run chill.   (39–44)

The poem continues in this melodramatic way through several hundred lines, although some are considerably better than those quoted. Blair's poem was not, as might be deduced, a poetic version of a 'horrid' novel but a poem of serious religious intent.

Yet another aspect of the poetic environment in which Wordsworth and Coleridge grew up was the revival of the ballad tradition. This movement was an outgrowth of the antiquarianism of the seventeenth century but its effect on literature was not felt until the mid-eighteenth century. Chatterton's forgeries (1763–70) and Macpherson's 'Ossian' (1760, 1762 and 1763), some of which was certainly fabricated, were both part of this mania. In Scotland an important figure was Burns (1759–96), who collected, revised and composed original folk-type songs. Wordsworth referred to both Chatterton and Burns in his poem 'Resolution and Independence', wrote several poems addressed to Burns and even apostrophised 'Ossian'. The most pervasive influence on both Wordsworth and Coleridge was Percy's *Reliques of Ancient English Poetry* (1765). It must be remembered, however, that the *Reliques* is a curiously miscellaneous collection. It consists of genuine old ballads and folksongs, such as the 'Ballad of Chevy Chace' and 'Barbara Allen', a number of compositions by known writers and numerous prose notes giving information about folk traditions. By the late 1790s what may be called 'ballad-fever' was raging through northern Europe. Many 'new' ballads were composed, especially in Germany and these were translated into English and printed in the literary papers of the day, such as *The Monthly Magazine*. Some, such as the ballads of Gottfried Burger (1747–94), were particularly popular in England and had a direct influence on Wordsworth and others. Burger's 'Leonore' (1774) was translated no fewer than five times, one version being by Sir Walter Scott, who, of course, both collected traditional Scottish ballads and composed ballads of his own.[4]

A further factor is the poetry of William Blake. Blake is sometimes called the first of the Romantic poets and his work greatly influenced Wordsworth, both in subject matter and form, as well as in the language in which it was written. Many of Blake's *Songs of Innocence* (1789) and *Songs of Experience* (1794) are written in simple stanzas and in a plain language quite unlike that of his predecessors and contemporaries.[5] The subject matter, too, particularly in *Songs of Experience*, is concerned with social evils and conditions that occupied the young Wordsworth. These had been anticipated to some extent in Goldsmith's *Deserted Village* (1770) and were also the subject of much of Crabbe's *The Village* (1783). Crabbe, however, was very much alone in his view of eighteenth-century life although his great poem is composed in a language and form which are firmly in the eighteenth-century mould.

Another influence on both Wordsworth and Coleridge was William Lisle Bowles (1762–1850). His *Fourteen Sonnets*, which were first published in 1789, were discovered by Coleridge while still a schoolboy at Christ's Hospital. He was so much taken with them that he made numerous copies to distribute among his friends. (*BL*, I, p. 7) The attention of Wordsworth, too, was so caught when he first saw them, probably during the Christmas Vacation of 1789–90, that he insisted on stopping in his walk across London Bridge and reading them straight through.[6] It may not be easy now for us to see very much difference between Bowles's manner of expression and that of many other eighteenth-century poets, but both Wordsworth and Coleridge detected in it a personalising of emotion and sincerity in its expression unknown before. A few lines will show the difference in attitude that attracted Wordsworth and Coleridge:

> I may look back on every sorrow past,
> And meet life's peaceful evening with a smile: –
>   As some lone bird, at day's departing hour,
>   Sings in the sunbeam, of the transient shower
> Forgetful, though its wings are wet the while.

The introduction of the first person pronoun is itself significant for its personalising effect; the designation of the 'lone bird' as *some* indicates an individual if unspecified bird; and the inclusion of the word *every* before *sorrow* also removes that emotion from a mere abstraction to a series of, again unspecified, but nevertheless specific, events. The lack of 'specificity' allows the reader to identify with the feeling of the poem through his own individual experiences, even though the poems are usually related to particular places, a practice that Wordsworth was also to follow. These linguistic points, small as they may seem, help to convey a sense of genuineness of emotion, which Bowles was anxious to make clear was 'natural' and not 'fabricated'.[7] This is also enhanced by the movement of the verse, which does not have the effect of such an emphatically finished statement as the heroic couplet does. The syntax has been loosened by the inclusion of prepositional phrases, such as 'at day's departing hour', between subject and verb, and of subordinate clauses, dependent upon and following the main statement, such as that in the last line here. This is much the same type of sentence structure that Wordsworth was to adopt in his own sonnets and blank verse poems. It introduces a leisurely, reflective tempo into the lines. This is particularly clear in the dying cadence produced by the final clause in the stanza quoted above. In other ways, such as the use of the classifying definite article before *sunbeam* and *shower*, Bowles is still writing in the eighteenth-century tradition. (See pp. 11–12 below.)

When it comes to verse forms used by the poets of the eighteenth century most people think automatically of the heroic couplet. By writing his two earliest poems of any importance in couplets, Wordsworth suggests that this was the principal verse form at the time. It certainly enjoyed great popularity and was well-suited to contemporary expression, but poets wrote in many other forms as well. James Thomson wrote *The Seasons* in blank verse and *The Castle of Indolence* in Spenserean stanzas. Collins and Gray both wrote in the irregular metrical form of the ode and Gray wrote his famous 'Elegy' in four-line stanzas. Many poets continued the lyric forms made popular by the Elizabethans. While we associate the century with the couplet, therefore, it is necessary to remember that this was not the only form in use.

Discussions of the language of eighteenth-century poetry are usually confined to 'poetic diction'. This can be misleading, since other factors enter into the matter besides vocabulary. The fault may lie partly with Wordsworth for his continual use of the term in his Prefaces, as well as in the Appendix of 1802, which deals wholly with this one subject. True, certain words are associated with the poetry of this period but they can almost all be found in earlier as well as later poetry, including that of Wordsworth and Coleridge. Combinations or collocations of certain words are equally, if not more, important. Pope summed it up as early as 1711 in his 'Essay on Criticism', when he wrote:

> Where-e'er you find 'the cooling western breeze,'
> In the next line, it 'whispers through the trees:'
> If crystal streams 'with pleasing murmurs creep,'
> The reader's threaten'd (not in vain) with 'sleep'.

This is, of course, partly a matter of rhyme, but 'brooks' are invariably 'babbling'; 'lawns' are 'dewy'; and 'woods', and many other objects, 'sylvan'.

Although it is almost always possible to identify an eighteenth-century poem by its language, its distinguishing quality is difficult to pin-point. Whatever criteria one suggests will not apply to all poems, but a few points can be made. Combinations of words frequently come in the composition of nominal groups.[8] Most nominal groups are relatively simple but nearly all nouns are premodified by an adjective, as in 'dewy lawn'; 'liquid sky'; 'quiv'ring shade'; 'well-breathed beagles'; and so on. These are all from Pope's *Windsor-Forest*. Compound adjectives, as in the last example here, are quite common, as are compound words generally. Coleridge has much to say on the subject of 'double epithets', which, in general, he believes should be avoided. (*BL*, I, p. 2, n. 1)[9] Nevertheless, they can be striking, as is the verb in the following from Thomson's 'Winter':

> a blackening Train
> Of clam'rous Rooks thick-urge their weary Flight.

Very many adjectives were formed from a noun with the

addition of the suffix –*y* as in *glassy*, *breezy*, and even such curiosities as *tusky*. The constant premodification of nouns by placing an adjective in front of them is so predictable in some poets (Thomson is an instance) that it becomes monotonous. Thomson is also full of periphrases, another feature common in much early eighteenth-century poetry. A periphrasis is a combination of words, usually an adjective and noun, that defines some particular characteristic of the natural object denoted without naming it. Examples from Thomson are *frosty tribe* for 'stinging insects'; *soft fearful people* for 'sheep'; *plumy people* for 'birds' (Thomson has very many different periphrases for birds); and *brittle bondage* for 'eggshells', when referring to the hatching of young birds.

Another feature of eighteenth-century poetry is the abstract manner in which much of it is expressed. Apart from a prolific use of abstract words, this is particularly effected by the profusion of personifications. The passage of the eighteenth century into the nineteenth has been called one of transition from the 'abstract' to the 'concrete'.[10] Generalisation is closely related to the abstract and various means of generalising were employed. One of the most common was the use of the plural form of a noun rather than the singular which would indicate that a specific object was in the poet's mind.

One generally unnoticed linguistic feature, although it is all-pervasive, is a particular use of the definite article *the* before certain types of nouns. Again this is frequent in Thomson and can be demonstrated from *The Seasons*:

> The blackbird whistles from the thorny brake,
> The mellow bullfinch answers from the grove;
> ......The jay, the rook, the daw,
> And each harsh pipe, discordant heard alone,
> Aid the full concert; while the stock-dove breathes
> A melancholy murmur through the whole. ('Spring', 604–13)

The definite article itself has no semantic content. Usually it 'indicates that the item in question is specific and identifiable'.[11] Here, however, the various birds denoted are clearly not specific. The definite article can be used to show that the object denoted has only one referent, for example 'the moon'; or that it refers to a whole class, for example 'the stars'; or that the individual is considered as a representative of the whole class, for example 'the snail' in 'The snail is considered a great delicacy in this region.'[11] This final usage, which is relatively uncommon in present-day literary English, is very frequent in eighteenth-century poetry and is part of its generalising manner of expression. It is what is called the 'classifying' use of the definite article.

Although most of these linguistic features can be found in Wordsworth's early poems, *An Evening Walk* (1787–9) and *Descriptive Sketches* (1791–2), and to a certain extent in 'The Female Vagrant' (1791–4), they tend later to disappear. They were the features of diction to which he objected in the Appendix to the 1800 Preface. The Lake District that is celebrated in *An Evening Walk* is so much in the eighteenth-century style that it may be difficult for us to recognise as the particular locality with which we are familiar. As in the graphic arts, painting and, more recently, photography, we see what we are conditioned to see by artistic representations. Wordsworth, along with painters such as Constable, was later to alter our perceptions to the extent that we now recognise the landscape of that part of the country as it appears in 'Michael' or 'The Brothers'. Coleridge seems to have detected a change of style already taking place in *Descriptive Sketches*, although it should be remembered that he saw this before *An Evening Walk*. In *Biographia Literaria* he says:

> In the form, style and manner of the whole poem, and in the structure of the particular lines and periods, there is a harshness and acerbity connected and combined with words and images...

and:

> The language was not only peculiar and strong, but at times knotty and contorted...
> (*BL*, IV, p. 46)

Although he complained that this made for obscurity, Coleridge also believed that it heralded the arrival of a poetic greatness. There are, perhaps, some slight indications of a shift towards

Wordsworth's later style, both in diction and syntax, in *Descriptive Sketches* but the expression of the first version, published in 1793, is still very much in the eighteenth-century style.

At the same time as he was engaged upon *Descriptive Sketches* Wordsworth began to write the poem he called 'Salisbury Plain'. The subject matter was influenced by his humanitarian sympathies as well as by his political leanings at the time. From this poem the lines that make up 'The Female Vagrant' were extracted to be included in the first edition of *Lyrical Ballads* in 1798. Not only was Wordsworth interested in the lives and hardships of humbler people, but because of his background he took his characters from rural life. 'Salisbury Plain', along with 'The Ruined Cottage', which he began in 1797, was partly intended to expose the evils of war, but the Vagrant herself is the daughter of a shepherd who has been forced to leave his home by a cruel landlord. As a consequence she undergoes many trials and is finally destitute. Later, Wordsworth was to describe some of the diction of this poem as 'vicious' and, indeed, he continually altered and revised the whole, never reaching a conclusion that wholly satisfied him even by the time it was finally published in its entirety as *Guilt and Sorrow* in 1842. In 'The Female Vagrant', nevertheless, the change in subject-matter and style, including diction, is quite clear.

All poets must, or should, be interested in language, which is the medium of their work, but few have written more on the subject than either Wordsworth or Coleridge. Wordsworth's Prefaces and other matter associated with *Lyrical Ballads* are well known and easily accessible. The Preface of 1800 was written at the insistence of Coleridge but there is no doubt that it embodies Wordsworth's own ideas on language as used in poetry. In addition, comments on language are scattered throughout his prose writings. Coleridge's *Biographia Literaria* (1817), which contains criticism of Wordsworth's poetic usages, is the best known of his works that deals with language, although it covers much else besides. However, Coleridge wrote many other mainly philosophical treatises and essays that contain reflections on language and some of his ideas are surprisingly modern. He realised, for instance, that different language is required for different subjects, or what would now be called 'registers', and he experimented in transferring the language of one register to another. Much of *Biographia Literaria* is written in the scientific language of the time.[12] It is not the purpose of this book, however, to discuss Wordsworth and Coleridge's ideas about language but to examine the language they used in their own poetry.

2 Experimental Narrative Ballads

In 'The Female Vagrant', written between 1791 and 1792, Wordsworth had found the subject matter that he wanted but he had still to find the medium in which to convey it. This he developed in a group of poems, all in some form of ballad measure and mostly written during the prolific year 1798. The language Wordsworth used for all these ballads is basically similar and marks a clear break from that which he used earlier and also, to some extent, that which he used later. It was influenced very greatly by the ballads of Percy's *Reliques* and the broadsheet ballads of the time.[1] In it, Wordsworth set himself severe limitations. He deliberately worked within a very restricted language, in both vocabulary and sentence structure, abandoning everything that had hitherto been associated with poetry, except rhyme and metre. There are difficulties in coming to terms with this language. Wordsworth uses both diction and syntax in such a new and bold manner that it sometimes hovers on the borders of collapse into the ludicrous even today. Nevertheless, its success in terms of what Wordsworth was trying to do is quite astonishing. Frequently it strikes readers who come fresh to it, with inbuilt assumptions of what to expect from poetry, as clumsy and banal. It is interesting, however, that a spoken performance has a quite different effect from a silent reading. When read aloud, 'The Thorn', for instance, can hold an audience spellbound, mesmerised by the sheer force of its linguistic effects, whereas a silent reading of the poem might evoke a response of bewilderment, mirth or even contempt. One of Wordsworth's most amazing feats in these experimental ballads is that he rarely uses the basic components of the language to which he has

15

restricted himself in exactly the same way in different poems.

The features of the language that all the experimental ballads have in common are fairly easily described. The vocabulary is largely monosyllabic or composed of derivatives from monosyllabic stems. In the main it derives from the original stock of Old English words. When words of Romance, usually French, origin, such as *infant* and *reason*, are used they are those that were borrowed very early in the history of the English language and have become so fully anglicised that their foreign origin is no longer felt. There is an abundance of nouns in the poems, mostly concrete, denoting objects that are part of the natural landscape or the elements: rocks and other physical features, names of animals, plants and trees, wind, sky, clouds, stars, states of weather and other similar natural or elemental and cosmic forces. Typical Wordsworthian synonyms, such as *eminence* for a hill or *torrent* or *cascade* for waterfall are notably absent. The abstract nouns that are found usually denote commonly felt emotions such as grief and patience. Verbs are generally less forceful than nouns and there is frequent use of grammatical or lexically empty verbs like the verb *to be* and verbs denoting states rather than actions.[2] Because of this, when Wordsworth does use a verb denoting a physical action it is all the more striking. In 'Simon Lee', for example, the mattock *totters* in the old man's hand. This is the one dynamic finite verb in this poem. In 'Goody Blake and Harry Gill' the dynamic verb *chatter* is part of the repetition in that poem, and helps to create an incantatory effect. Adjectives are on the whole rather conventional and commonplace. Examples are *comely*; *fair*; *sad*; *happy*; and *lovely*. Because of their very ordinariness, Wordsworth can use them to good effect by stepping only very slightly outside his usual run. In 'The Thorn' the use of colour adjectives in the description of the 'hill of moss', allegedly the child's grave, is remarkably vivid and memorable in context. Simple colours, such as *green* and *red*, take on a brilliance not usually theirs, especially in conjunction with the less usual *vermilion* and the word *dye*, which is part of the simile in which they all occur:

All lovely colours there you see,
All colours that were ever seen,

And mossy network too is there,
As if by hand of lady fair
The work had woven been.
And cups, the darlings of the eye
So deep in their vermilion dye.

Ah me! what lovely tints are there!
Of olive-green and scarlet bright,
In spikes, in branches, and in stars,
Green, red, and pearly white.

The syntax is similarly limited in its range of structures. Most clauses are short, running to two lines at most, and the lines also are short, consisting mainly of eight syllables. Just a few clauses, in certain poems, are longer. Most clauses are self-contained sentences or if linked to another clause in a clause complex[3] are joined by a co-ordinate conjunction, such as *but*; *for* or, most usual, *and*. Subordinate clauses are few and such as do exist are restricted to the simpler *if* and *when* type, as for example:

Whene'er you look on it, 'tis plain
The baby looks at you again.

or:

When he was young he little knew
Of husbandry or tillage.

A somewhat longer and more complex example, from 'The Last of the Flock' is:

When I was young, a single man,
And after youthful follies ran,
Though little given to care and thought,
Yet, so it was, a ewe I bought.

But this is a typical deviation from the norm that occurs in this poem and is suited to its particular narrator. Even so, the first subordinate clause occupies one line, as does the concessive clause of the third line, a more unusual type of clause for these ballads. The holding up of the main statement here until the second half of the fourth line is also unusual though crucial for the meaning of this particular poem. Important, too, is the inversion of the usual order, with the ewe, the complement,[3] placed before the subject. This type of inversion is one of the few devices that Wordsworth allows himself. In general the word order of clauses is S V C A, with occasionally the A placed first, as in '*Up to the mountain top* she goes.' [My italics.] The first line of each clause frequently contains S V C and if the clause extends to a second line that takes the form of an expansion of the C element. Sometimes it is simply another complement in apposition to the first:

It is a mass of knotted joints,
A wretched thing forlorn.

At other times the second line contains a co-ordinate complement:

The winds at night had made a rout,
And scatter'd many a lusty splinter,
And many a rotten bough about.

Here 'many a rotten bough' is a separate complement co-ordinate with 'a lusty splinter'. An expansion of a complement comes in:

And close beside this aged thorn,
There is a fresh and lovely sight,
A beauteous heap, a hill of moss,
Just half a foot in height.

There are three complements in apposition: the 'fresh and lovely sight', the 'beauteous heap' and the 'hill of moss'. The final line of the quotation is an expansion of all three. A postmodification of an adjectival complement is fairly frequent, as in the following, in which *o'ergrown* is an adjective complement:

Like rock or stone, it is o'ergrown
With lichens to the very top. [My italics]

Less common is the more complex type of expansion seen later
in this same stanza where the verbal group *were bent* is followed
first by an adverbial adjunct, which takes up a full line, and
then by a non-finite clause in the final line:

Up from the earth these mosses creep,
And this poor thorn they clasp it round
So close, you'd say that they were bent
With plain and manifest intent,
To drag it to the ground.

This slight degree of syntactical complexity is one of the
features of this poem that mark it out from the other narrative
ballads.

One syntactical device that Wordsworth uses occasionally in
many of the ballads is that of thematic marking. This happens
when a clause element other than the normal subject comes
first in the clause and thereby focuses the reader's attention on
it. Whatever element is placed first in a clause is called the
theme and this carries the main part of the 'message' or
meaning. It is what the sentence is about. When the subject (or
S element) is first, the clause or sentence is said not to be
thematically marked, since this is the usual and expected order.
In theory any element may be placed first but in practice it is
very unusual for the verb to appear in this position and not
very common for the complement, although the latter is found
more often in poetry than in written prose or conversation.
The most frequent thematic marking is that of an adverbial or
A element. At times, in poetry, this may seem no more than a
matter of metrical arrangement or even a more natural order,
although thematic marking always has an effect on the meaning
or emphasis of the sentence.[4] One example has already been
quoted: 'a ewe I bought' from 'The Last of the Flock'. Here,
the complement is marked. The less likely an element is to be in
the marked position, the more 'powerful' is the marking. It is
easy to see how important the inversion is for the meaning of
the narrative here. The 'ewe' is the first sheep of the flock that

the shepherd has built up only to lose it again, until he is seen by the narrator carrying the 'last' lamb. Another example is found in 'The Mad Mother' when the mother, addressing her infant son, says:

> Then do not fear, my boy! for thee
> Bold as a lion I will be.

Elsewhere, this poem is extremely straightforward, following normal word order, with unmarked themes, and the clauses are mostly short. Just occasionally Wordsworth introduces a marked theme as here: 'for thee', an A element. In addition there is an inversion after the marked theme: 'Bold as a lion'; the C with its included simile comes before S and V. The marked theme and the preplaced adjectival complement indicate the thoughts uppermost in the mother's mind: first, her baby (the stress on *thee* is further emphasised by its falling at the end of the line and in rhyming position), and second, her protective attitude towards him – 'Bold as a lion'. The simple statement, 'I will be', merely affirms or predicates the mother's attitude to her son. The focus of attention here, then, is (1) the baby; (2) the mother and her feelings towards her child. This, basically, is the essential meaning of the poem and it is, perhaps, not without importance that this, the main thematically marked statement, comes roughly in the middle, at the very heart of the poem. The more common type of thematically marked adverbial group element concerns time and it occurs in large numbers in 'The Thorn', as do thematically marked independent clauses of time. The reason for this is again closely bound up with the atmosphere of this particular poem.

Another device which Wordsworth may have copied from the broadsheet ballads is change of tense. This is usually from the simple past to the present, occasionally an expanded or continuous present, during the course of the narration. This use of the so-called 'historic' present is dramatic and conveys a sense of immediacy to the narrative. One example that occurs at a crucial point in the poem is the following from 'Goody Blake and Harry Gill':

> And once, behind a rick of barley,
> Thus looking out did Harry stand;

The moon was full and shining clearly,
And crisp with frost the stubble-land.
– He hears a noise – he's all awake –
Again? – on tip-toe down the hill
He softly creeps – 'Tis Goody Blake,
She's at the hedge of Harry Gill.

The next stanza reverts to the past tense. This is not the main climax of the poem, which is expressed in the past, but comes just before, at the point where the young farmer is about to discover Goody Blake stealing wood from his hedge. It raises the excitement and dramatic tension at the point which leads on to the climactic curse. There are numerous other instances in the poems.

Wordsworth was probably referring at least partly to the personification in 'The Female Vagrant' when he described its language as 'vicious', and personification is not found in these ballads. Some figurative language, however, is traditionally associated with the speech of ordinary folk, most notably perhaps the use of proverbs or proverbial-type sayings. There are occasional proverbial-type lines in these ballads, such as 'The pony's worth his weight in gold', from 'The Idiot Boy'. There is nothing very remarkable in this everyday idiom and it is one that might be expected to occur on the lips of the characters in this poem, where a more than average number of them occur. Apart from these, Wordsworth does allow himself some other figures of speech but they are again rigorously limited. The most common are short and often common-place similes, like 'bold as a lion'. The object to which something is likened is often an unmodified, concrete noun. In 'Simon Lee' the only simile refers to the old man, whose 'cheek is like a cherry' and in 'The Thorn' the wind 'cuts like a scythe'. 'The Thorn', again, is something of an exception as it contains considerably more similes than the other ballads, and one even moves away from natural objects for comparison. When the narrator describes the appearance of the hill of moss he likens it to a lady's tapestry. Metaphors are even rarer than similes. When they do occur, they are brought in almost obliquely, as in the voices of 'the chiming hounds' in 'Simon Lee'. A figure of speech that Wordsworth uses frequently is that of apostrophe. This is found particularly in 'The Idiot Boy', where a number of apostrophes occur at the beginning, as the poet/narrator addresses the mother of the boy, and again when he invokes his muses. Even more frequent is his use of exclamation, examples of which can be easily found. These few figures of speech account for practically all the kinds that occur in these ballads.

One final linguistic device should be mentioned and it is not least in importance. This is the vast amount of repetition. It embraces not only vocabulary and syntax but can also be regarded as a kind of rhetorical or figurative device. Wordsworth runs the whole gamut of types of repetition, from single words to whole sentences. In between these two extremes come repeated phrases, repeated syntactical patterns with different words filling the various grammatical slots, and repeated rhymes. Again, with this apparently limited tool, one of the most difficult to use without falling into the trap of banality, Wordsworth achieves a surprising variety of effects.[5] The repetition of the word *baby* in 'The Thorn' conveys both a sense of horror and pathos:

> Some say, if to the pond you go,
> And fix on it a steady view,
> The shadow of a babe you trace,
> A baby and a baby's face.

Another example, with a slightly different kind of repetition, is found in 'Goody Blake and Harry Gill':

> And fiercely by the arm he took her,
> And by the arm he held her fast,
> And fiercely by the arm he shook her,
> And cried, 'I've caught you then at last!'

Here the syntactical pattern of the co-ordinate clauses is repeated until the final triumphant cry. There is repetition, too, of various key words and phrases. 'By the arm', used three times in three lines, emphasises the physical force the young farmer shows towards the defenceless old woman and the repetition of 'fiercely' further conveys his brutal attitude. The near repetition of the clauses: 'he took her'; 'he held her'; 'he shook her', with the first and third differing only in the initial sound of the verb, indicates the increasing violence of the farmer's actions. The farmer's violence is contrasted with the passiveness of his victim, 'who had nothing said'.

The metres of the experimental ballads are also of importance. Not surprisingly, Wordsworth uses the metre of the majority of traditional and broadsheet ballads which he took as his model. Blake, too, made use of such measures in his *Songs of Innocence* (1789), as did Isaac Watts much earlier in *Divine Hymns for Children* (1715). Blake was probably influenced by Watts as well as by the broadsheet ballads. Both of these titles indicate their association with simplicity (not to be mistaken for simple-mindedness) and childlike innocence and this undoubtedly affected Wordsworth's choice also, since it was the essential simplicity of the characters of his poems that he was anxious to convey. The stanza form varies from ballad to ballad, as do the rhyme schemes, some of which are fairly complex. The most common type of line is the strict ballad metre of a four-stress line, composed of iambs: v–v–v–v–. Inverted feet are rare. Occasionally, Wordsworth varies the line length to one of three stresses, especially in those ballads where the stanza is longer, such as 'The Thorn' and 'The Last of the Flock'. The brevity of the line length means that many lines contain a mere eight syllables, frequently eight monosyllabic words. This has two distinct effects, both of which Wordsworth exploited. The first is that the simple, short clauses, which constitute many of these lines, impart a speed to the narrative as statement follows statement in quick succession. This is reinforced by the occasional short line. This speed, however, is counterbalanced by the frequent repetitions, which have the effect of delaying or holding up the narrative, thus slowing down the pace of the story. That Wordsworth was alert to the effects of metre and also that he exploited it is known from his comment on 'The Thorn' in the Note of 1800:

It was necessary that the Poem, to be natural, should in reality move slowly; yet I hoped, that, by the aid of the metre, to those who should at all enter into the spirit of the Poem, it would appear to move quickly.   (*LB*, p. 288)

Wordsworth does not say exactly how he hopes to achieve this effect by means of the metre but it is clear that he believes it to be crucial.

Wordsworth chose for nearly every poem a different approach or kind of presentation. In some there is an external narrator, apparently impartial, as in 'The Idiot Boy' and 'Simon Lee'; in 'The Thorn' he employs a *persona*, a characterised narrator; and in others, such as 'The Mad Mother' and 'The Last of the Flock', the central character tells the tale after an initial introduction by a poet/narrator acting as an observer and interlocutor. Even within the narration of the tale Wordsworth causes the narrator, of whatever sort, to adopt different attitudes to the particular tale and its characters and this affects the way in which he deploys the language.

Of all his experiments in narrative ballad form 'Goody Blake and Harry Gill' is probably the most traditional. It is the nearest that Wordsworth approaches to pastiche of the broadsheet ballads. The tale is a straightforward narrative ballad and, while still using the same basic vocabulary and syntactical structures found in the other experimental ballads, it incorporates traditional ballad-type features, less noticeable in the other poems. One of these is the formulaic phrase associated with traditional ballads, such as:

His voice was *like the voice of three,*

and:

For they come far *by wind and tide.*　　　　　[My italics]

The curse, which is the climax of the poem, is itself a formula, both in wording and effect. Coleridge's ballad poems, *The Rime of the Ancyent Marinere* and *Christabel*, and also the lesser known *The Three Graves*, of which Wordsworth wrote part, all incorporate the curse of traditional ballads and it is, therefore, perhaps not surprising that 'Goody Blake and Harry Gill' is in places very close to the sort of wording found in these poems. The moral brought in explicitly at the end is also formulaic. It is reminiscent of such ballads as 'Barbara Allen' and also of the well-known carol, written in ballad metre and style, 'Good King

Wenceslas'. Read in this light, the apparent absurdity of the repetitive, 'His teeth they chatter, chatter still' becomes acceptable and even, in performance, sinister. Apart from this almost refrain-like repetition, there is less repetition of vocabulary here than in his other ballads. There is, however, repetition of phrase and clause patterns, such as:

Beneath the sun, beneath the moon,

or:

She left her fire, or left her bed.

There is also a repetitive quality about such doublets as 'well or sick' and 'cold and chill'. Repeated clause structures occur, one of which was examined earlier and leads up to the curse. This contains a series of co-ordinate clauses, and there is another cluster of these earlier, also describing the actions of the young farmer, Harry Gill. Even so, there are a number of longer and slightly more complicated sentences or clause complexes[3] than in most of the ballads. In spite of its conventional mode there are one or two vivid similes. The first two, describing Harry Gill, are in the traditional formula style. The farmer's cheeks are 'like ruddy clover' and 'His voice is like the voice of three'. Another, however, is more striking. Harry's chattering jaw is likened to 'a loose casement in the wind'. Even allowing for the fact that *casement* was a more common word then than now, the comparison is unusual and graphic. A fair number of weak or feminine rhymes occur throughout the poem. Indeed, the first pair of rhyming words in every stanza is of this type. In spite of the social comment that Wordsworth makes, he maintains a lightness of touch which is achieved partly through these rhymes, which often have a slightly comic sound in English. Again, as in the traditional ballads, Wordsworth changes tense from past to present at one of the dramatic points of the poem. This ballad, which was composed between March and early May of 1798, is probably the first experimental ballad that Wordsworth wrote.[6]

'The Idiot Boy' works on several levels at once and this Wordsworth achieves partly through language. Ostensibly, it has an external narrator, but the way in which this narrator tells the tale is extremely complex. It has been pointed out that the wording of the initial narrative stanza is probably intended to alert the reader to Wordsworth's intention to 'take off' the popular German contemporary Gothick ballad, in particular 'Leonore' by Burger.[7] Because of the numerous translations this would have been well known to Wordsworth's readers. This, then, sets the tone for the ensuing parody of the Gothick-type literature of the day, both prose and poetry. After this first stanza the poet/narrator directly addresses the mother, Betty Foy. First Wordsworth uses questions, then urges the mother to abandon her task in an imperative: 'Good Betty! put him down again'. His attitude of kindly good humour to the mother is conveyed by the use of her Christian name, coupled with the familiar tone of the word *good*, and the type of language one uses to a loved but naughty child: 'put him down'. This also hints at the attitude he adopts towards the boy himself: he is something that can be treated in this proprietary way, an object that can be moved from place to place, rather like a doll. This, however, is only one way in which Wordsworth depicts him. His attitude to the mother is further conveyed in the word *fiddle-faddle*:

> let Betty Foy
> With girt and stirrup fiddle-faddle.

The fidgetiness of the mother is neatly indicated through this one colloquial hybrid. Reduplicative words of this type, such as *tittle-tattle*, are associated with informal speech.

The use of *girt and stirrup* should be noticed,[8] because later Wordsworth casually lets slip the word *spur*. Its collocation with *boot*: 'There is no need of boot and spur', an instance of borrowing from the traditional ballad language, contrasts with the words he uses earlier, 'girt and stirrup'. These are from the everyday world of his characters; 'boot and spur' are from the register of courtly romance. Later, Wordsworth uses another word from this register, apparently by chance: 'His steed and he right well agree'. *Steed* is also from the romantic literary world. Wordsworth is mocking this type of literature but he also shows how the boy is the hero of a romance in his mother's eyes. This picture of Johnny reaches its climax in the stanza where the narrator shows him to the reader after the long night of his absence:

Who's yon, that, near the waterfall,
Which thunders down with headlong force,
Beneath the moon, yet shining fair,
As careless as if nothing were,
Sits upright on a feeding horse?

Apart from the setting by the waterfall, the description of which has a slightly Gothick aura, there is nothing that positively directs the reader to see Johnny as a heroic knight. However, that seems to be the picture intended. The careful placing of *shining* in 'shining fair' gives the impression of shining armour, although it is not explicitly stated. Similarly, the word *upright* is a word more suited to the hero of a romance than to an idiot boy. The game is given away and we are proved right in this reading by the following stanza:

Unto his horse, that's feeding free,
He seems, I think, the rein to give;
Of moon or stars he takes no heed;
Of such we in romances read.

The introduction of the word *romances* places Johnny once more in the world of *steeds* and *spurs*. In fact up to this point and by deferring the key word, Wordsworth has it both ways. The vocabulary used would not necessarily make the reader see the boy as anything other than he is; and it is only the earlier words that give the hint that there is another way of viewing him. Having re-introduced the notion of the romantic hero, Wordsworth immediately undermines it with the final line of the stanza: '– 'Tis Johnny! Johnny! as I live.' Again the use of the familiar Christian name together with the exclamations, conveys the teasing, familiar attitude of the narrator towards the hero and also indicates his mocking of romantic literature. As the omniscient narrator, he has, of course, known all along who it was.

The slight deviation from the usual diction in this ballad,

enables Wordsworth to establish his attitude of quizzical detachment towards the characters of his tale as well as to mock the type of literary genre which he has chosen to burlesque. Yet Wordsworth's amusement is by no means confined to the characters in the story or even to contemporary literature. He turns the mockery on himself (and perhaps poets as a race) when he upbraids his muses for deserting him and not allowing him to tell the adventures which Johnny is supposed to encounter on the Romantic/Gothick level of the burlesque:

> Oh gentle muses! is this kind?
> Why will ye thus my suit repel?
> Why of your further aid bereave me?

The language in these two stanzas sounds slightly more elevated, mostly through the use of apostrophe and to some extent through the diction. The word *suit* used in this sense, is not one that would be likely to occur in the speech of Betty Foy or Susan Gale, but it is a monosyllable and not particularly high-flown. *Bereave*, also, sounds more literary but is of Old English origin and is a word that might well be used by such people. It is still in common use today. The short question type sentences are reminiscent of the way the poet has previously addressed Betty and helps to place him on her level. The poetic and somewhat archaic use of the pronoun *ye* also gives an elevated tone to the passage, as does the C V inversion in 'my suit repel?', which is not dictated by considerations of rhyme. In the first of the two stanzas the word *indentures* in the lines:

> I to the muses have been bound,
> These fourteen years, by strong indentures,

also seems rather literary. Like *bereave*, however, it would have been well within the vocabulary of the class of people portrayed in these ballads. Even country lads were apprenticed by 'indentures'. The husband of the Female Vagrant was so apprenticed in the town. All these small points of diction and syntax, even when the literariness is more apparent than real, scarcely seem to be appropriate to the lowly subject to which the poet is addressing himself and further stress the mock solemnity which Wordsworth adopts at this point.

With a certain dexterity Wordsworth keeps the language within the range of the class of people with whom he is concerned and yet at the same time selects from that language in order to vary his meaning and effects. We see him doing this in the stanzas immediately preceding the address to the muses, where he is attempting to describe the kind of adventures Johnny is supposed to have met with:

> He with his pony now doth roam
> The cliffs and peaks so high that are,
> To lay his hands upon a star,
> And in his pocket bring it home.

The grandeur and vastness of the natural scene is sketched in lightly with the nouns *peaks* and *cliffs* together with the adjective *high*; and then the cosmic plane is introduced, as so often in Wordsworth's poetry, with the single word *star*. The curious inversion of the line before emphasises the daring and breath-taking simplicity of the short unqualified clause 'To lay his hands upon a star'. This is the language of visionary madness appropriate to the mad boy. Wordsworth quickly follows this by bringing us down to earth with the everyday words *pocket* and *home* in an almost equally simple clause. Indeed the thematic marking in this clause serves to throw the very ordinary noun *pocket* into prominence and also to contrast it by juxtaposition with the vision of seizing a star from the sky. Just after these lines, Johnny is portrayed as a 'fierce and dreadful hunter', but we discover that it is not the dragons or knights of romance that he is hunting but simply the sheep of his native hills. Even the image of the 'desert wilderness' that he will create, although not the language normally used in these ballads, would be within the competence of ordinary folk, since it is the language of the Bible, a book which of all others they would have known best. Similarly, when Betty herself speaks of the horrors she fears may have befallen Johnny, Wordsworth puts into her mouth words that are not part of the basic vocabulary to which he limits himself in writing these ballads. She speaks of goblins, castles and ghosts, the vocabulary of the superstitions she, in common with other women of her type, would have held:

> Or him that wicked pony's carried
> To the dark cave, the goblins' hall,
> Or in the castle he's pursuing,
> Among the ghosts, his own undoing.

As well as superstition, this is the language of the broadsheet ballad. This is not the place to go into the question of how far the rural population could read these ballads that were then circulating at fairs and other gatherings.[9] It is sufficient to note that Betty would have known the tales they told, and so this language would have been familiar to her. Again the type of vocabulary used at this point is nearer to that used by Coleridge in *The Ancyent Marinere* and *Christabel*. This is no accident since his ballads were based on the supernatural which was the subject-matter of these traditional ballads. The use of the definite articles in such phrases as 'the dark cave' and 'the goblins' hall' may mean that Wordsworth intended Betty to be thinking of one particular ballad which she believed to be literally true, or perhaps different ballads simply created one world for her. Whichever it is, Wordsworth contrives in this way to convey a sense of her naïvety. The stanza finishes with the line:

> Or playing with the waterfall.

This seems to be a reversion to the actual region which they inhabit but the use of the word *waterfall* is significant. Wordsworth uses it on more than one occasion in this poem but when describing the scene where Betty is re-united with her son, he steps briefly right outside the language of ordinary life and uses the more poetic *torrent*:

> She darts as with a torrent's force.

Moreover, the unusual word is embodied in a simile. In this way Wordsworth exaggerates the joy with which Betty greets her son. In the following line he returns to the everyday language, although it is no less hyperbolic and this, coupled with the juxtaposition of the two levels of language, renders its exaggeration ridiculously comic:

She almost has o'erturned the horse.

Most of Wordsworth's variations in diction to achieve his particular ends have been based on single, mostly unmodified, nouns. Occasionally he draws on adjectives or more lexically empty words, such as pronouns, to add to the force of these. On the whole, the introduction of vocabulary not normally used in these ballads is so slight and so deftly done that it is easy to overlook and thereby to miss the shifts in viewpoint that Wordsworth intends. These are never inadvert or without meaning for the poem and it is important that the reader is constantly alert to detect anything unusual in the language.

The syntax of 'The Idiot Boy' also has its own particular characteristics. The most obvious is the abundance of very short phrases and even clauses. Wordsworth frequently breaks up a line, or several lines in succession, into two halves. At times he goes still further and has four separate, usually parallel, constructions in one line. The first of these occurs as Betty sets her son on his way:

And he must post without delay
Across the bridge that's in the dale,
And by the church, and o'er the down,
To bring a doctor from the town.

Here, the third is the only split line. The two halves constitute the second and third qualifying adverbial phrases relating to place of the verbal group *must post*. Combined with the co-ordinating conjunction *and*, used three times, they give an impression of breathlessness and seem to represent Betty's hurried instructions. It is a type of indirect speech, reflecting the agitation of the speaker through the accumulated adverbial qualifiers of the verb. The feeling that this is representation of actual speech is further enhanced by the final line of the stanza:

Or she will die, old Susan Gale.

This final naming of Susan Gale, who is referred to by the pronoun *she* placed earlier in the sentence is a common feature of speech. It occurs because speakers are so preoccupied with whatever they are speaking of that they automatically use a pronoun, assuming that it is also obvious to the listener. Then, realising that it may not be, the speaker tacks on the referent of the pronoun at the end of the sentence for clarification, as here. The postponed word referring back is almost always a noun or proper name. When using direct speech in quotation marks, Wordsworth is often not so convincing at reproducing the effect of real speech, but here, in what is to all intents and purposes indirect speech, he catches perfectly the normal speech characteristics and conveys with a sure ear the urgency of the mother's anxious instructions.

Another example of the syntax reflecting Betty's state of mind, which again works up to a split line, containing two short, contrastive clauses, is the following:

> And Susan's growing worse and worse,
> And Betty's in a sad quandary;
> And then there's nobody to say
> *If she must go or she must stay;*
> – She's in a sad quandary.   [My italics]

The agitation of Betty's thoughts is conveyed once again through the proliferation of the co-ordinate conjunctions, the repeated *worse and worse* and the conversational *And then*, where formal English would perhaps have *moreover* or, nowadays, *furthermore*. An added feature here is the word *quandary*. Clearly, Wordsworth intends to convey the older pronunciation with the stress on the second syllable.[10] Either his own pronunciation was rather old-fashioned or, more likely, he intended that Betty's should be. Either way it distorts the metrical pattern of the line. The very repetition of it as the rhyming word for itself shows that the poet intended to draw attention to it. Whatever the pronunciation, it is certain that the confusion in Betty's mind is mirrored in that of the reader as he hesitates over how to pronounce the word, although we cannot be sure that this effect was intended by the poet.

Wordsworth also uses the device of breaking the lines to reflect physical movement, as when Betty goes in search of Johnny:

So, through the moonlight lane she goes,
And far into the moonlight dale;
And how she ran, and how she walked,
And all that to herself she talked,
Would surely be a tedious tale.

The co-ordinate conjunctions appear in greater numbers than usual, helping to create the sense of agitation and nervous worry of Betty's progress. The most striking stanza showing this division of lines occurs immediately after this:

In high and low, above, below,
In great and small, in round and square,
In tree and tower was Johnny seen,
In bush and brake, in black and green.
'Twas Johnny, Johnny, every where.

Here, three of the five lines are divided into four parts, each consisting of only one word, which is the complement of the preposition *in*. As prepositional complements are invariably nouns or pronouns, it is apparent that the majority of these words are transferred parts of speech, that is adjectives or adverbs functioning as nouns. Since Wordsworth does not make any great use of the facility of English to transfer one part of speech to another, and he uses a greater number of concrete nouns than usual in these experimental ballads, the result is even more striking than it would otherwise be. The words *round* and *square* could be either nouns or adjectives, but if they are nouns they are abstract ones. What, then, is the effect and what is Wordsworth attempting to do here? It could be that in her anxious searching hither and thither for her son Betty's vision becomes blurred and the concrete objects of the landscape dissolve into mere shapes and colours. That at least is the notion presented to us by the poet. It conveys a strange scene that is, in effect, a series of impressions that pass rapidly in front of the eye.

Changing tense is another of the syntactical devices that Wordsworth uses. Here, the poem starts in the present tense and rather unusually shifts to the past. Then for a short while it alternates between past and present, using also the present perfect and continuous present tenses. In spite of the rather wider than usual variety of tense forms that Wordsworth draws on, the greater part of the poem is in the simple present. The whole narrative is presented dramatically and so the present tense is appropriate. The occasional use of the present continuous tense makes the scene even more immediate to the reader, as in the first line of:

> And Betty's *standing* at the door,
> And Betty's face with joy o'erflows.   [My italics]

Although the active forms of the continuous tenses were fully established in English by this time, Wordsworth uses them relatively infrequently and hardly ever, except in this poem, when recording the actions of human beings.

Even within the simple present we are sometimes aware of a shift from the narrator's comment to the actual perceptions of the mother:

> The silence of her idiot boy,
> What hopes it sends to Betty's heart!
> He's at the guide post – he turns right,
> She watches till he's out of sight.

Here, with the broken line brought into play again, we are aware that this is Betty herself, anxiously watching her son to see that he takes the right way. At times it is difficult to distinguish the narrator's comment from Betty's speech or thoughts, so completely are the two integrated. In the description of the horse we find:

> For of this pony there's a rumour,
> That should he lose his eyes and ears,
> And should he live a thousand years,
> He never will be out of humour.
>
> But then he is a horse that thinks!

Is this the narrator, or Betty reassuring Susan Gale of the reliability of Johnny's mount? In the last line especially it is impossible to be sure whether it is Betty in all seriousness or the narrator speaking with affectionate and fantastic good humour.

One example of thematic marking has already been mentioned. There is another very striking example clearly related to the meaning. This occurs just after Johnny has been seen safely on his way for the doctor. For a few moments, before she begins to worry at his non-return, Betty rests secure in her faith in her son. The stanza starts by stating this explicitly:

> And Betty's still at Susan's side:
> By this time she's not quite so flurried.

Then comes the change of normal word order that marks the theme of the following statement:

> Demure with porringer and plate
> She sits.

'She sits with porringer and plate / Demure' would have fitted the metre just as well, which makes it seem an even clearer example of deviation from normal word order on the poet's part. Certainly, it has the effect of throwing the focus of the reader on the marked word *Demure*. We are forced to recognise the complacency and confidence which Betty now feels in her son.[11] The sense of relaxed tension is further attained by the rare run-on line. This temporarily halts the galloping rhythm of the four stresses and dissipates the energy of the first line into the next, coming to rest at the strongly marked pause after the main verb *sits*.

Nowhere does Wordsworth's affectionate attitude towards his characters make itself more apparent than in the lines:

> The owls have hardly sung their last,
> While our four travellers homeward wend.

How many readers, I wonder, pass over this second line without realising that Wordsworth has included the pony in the 'merry meeting' – the 'horse that thinks!' It is indicative not only of his good-humoured treatment of the tale but also of the sympathy that ensures it is not merely a comic poem but one behind the surface humour of which lies a deep seriousness and compassion for the mental states of all sorts and conditions of people.

In 'The Last of the Flock' Wordsworth uses the same basic vocabulary and syntactic structures as those used in 'The Idiot Boy' but this time with a completely different effect. Here, the main narrator of the poem is the shepherd himself. The poet merely introduces him in the first two stanzas and prompts him to tell his tale. Whereas in 'The Idiot Boy' the two women, however sympathetically Wordsworth entered into their predicament, were simply two agitated simple women, the shepherd in this poem is not only a man of some substance, in spite of his lowly occupation, but, more important, he has an innate dignity, which demonstrates itself through the stateliness of the language he uses. So Wordsworth contrasts the moithered, almost comic, distress of the women with the tragic dignity of the man, and does this with virtually the same linguistic tools.

First, we should note that he varies the metre slightly. Wordsworth made a great point of the importance of metre in the Preface of 1800. Indeed, he implies that poetry is virtually prose expressed metrically:

> it would be a most easy task to prove ... that not only the language of a large portion of every good poem, even of the most elevated character, must necessarily, except with reference to the metre, in no respect differ from that of good prose, but likewise that some of the most interesting parts of the best poems will be found to be strictly the language of prose when prose is well written.   (LB, p. 252)

It is the metre and choice of metre, rather than all the other artificialities of language usually associated with poetry, that make it essentially different from prose. Wordsworth is not being dismissive of poetry here, as might at first be thought, but stressing the basic importance of metrical arrangement in the poet's craft. 'The Idiot Boy' was in quatrains of four-stress lines, all made up of four iambs: v–v–v–v–. The rhyme scheme was a simple ballad-type scheme of abab. 'The Last of the Flock' is far more complicated. The stanzas are ten lines in length with a complex rhyme scheme, especially in the middle of each stanza: aa bb cded ff. Each line again has four stresses with the exception of one three-stressed line. This falls on the second of the one split pair of rhyming lines, that is line 7. This placing of the short line near the end of the stanza throws it into prominence, since by this time the reader is expecting four stresses. Frequently, the short line falls at the end of a clause and has the effect of suggesting reticence on the narrator's part, as if he were holding something back. It is not too fanciful to say that it produces the sense of a lump in the throat, which the shepherd overcomes as he finishes the stanza with a two line couplet. The 'silent' stress of the short line lends a tragic dignity to the shepherd's narration. This short line is frequently run on from the line before, so that it has the effect of being part of a fuller statement as well as not fulfilling the expectation of the reader. Thus, the jogtrot, hypnotic four-stress rhythm is broken at regular intervals. The sense of shape this gives to the shepherd's speech heightens the tragedy of his tale. This can be seen in even a short extract:

> God cursed me in my sore distress,
> I prayed, yet every day I thought
> I loved my children less.

The vocabulary is not quite so monosyllabic as that of 'The Idiot Boy' and others of the narrative ballads. Wordsworth uses here a fair sprinkling of disyllabic words, although they originate from the same common core of English vocabulary. There are, perhaps, more abstract nouns, such as *grief*; *labour*; *peace*; *comfort*, and so on. Dynamic or 'action' verbs are less frequent than usual, with the exception of one or two (most notably the oft-repeated *dwindled*) and the dynamic verbs that do occur are commonplace, such as *bought* and *sold*. Verbs of inert perception, such as *see* and *think* are, conversely, frequent, and lexically empty and copula verbs like *be* and *seem* appear in large numbers. The sense of energy or agitation, so prominent, even if misdirected, in 'The Idiot Boy' is entirely absent. 'I went my work about' may seem an unnecessary circumlocution but, apart from fitting the rhyme, it helps to dissipate the energy of the shorter and more normal 'I worked'. It matches the lethargy or despair of the shepherd at this point:

> And crazily, and wearily,
> I went my work about.

Note here, too, the thematic marking of the two adverbs of manner, which emphasises the apathetic frame of mind into which the shepherd has fallen.

In this poem a verb is also occasionally omitted altogether, as in part of the description of the gradual selling of the flock, where only one finite verb occurs in four lines:

> They dwindled, Sir, sad sight to see!
> From ten to five, from five to three,
> A lamb, a wether, and a ewe;
> And then at last, from three to two.

The shepherd is a resigned figure, beaten by the society he lives in as much as by natural causes, and he has become passive, a fact that is conveyed not by the use of the passive voice, as it might have been, but by the non-dynamic and lexically empty verbs and, at times, by an absence of verbs altogether.

Apart from the ellipted verbs, the sentence structure is straightforward with very little inversion. It is the syntax of simple statement, the very simplicity giving added dignity to the story. The singular lack of energy and the flatness of the language might make the shepherd seem a weak or shadowy character, but Wordsworth gives some poetic heightening to his speech that counteracts any such impression. He does this mainly in two ways: the use of similes and the use of repetition, both usual features of these ballads but here employed in a way characteristic of this poem alone. There are, in fact, only two similes, but these are both vivid and appropriate to the shepherd. The first is contained in a single line:

> To see it melt like snow away.

The shepherd is, of course, referring to his flock. The second runs across two lines and again refers to the diminishing flock:

> It was a vein that never stopp'd,
> Like blood-drops from my heart they dropp'd.

Here, there is repetition of the word *drop*. Although only the significant word *melt* from the first quotation is repeated in the following lines, the images seem to haunt the rest of the poem. Certainly, the sense, which they convey so vividly, is the whole matter of the shepherd's story. Both are simple similes, drawn from natural life and well within the shepherd's range of experience. They are nevertheless forceful, partly perhaps through their association with the colours white and red, symbolic of innocence and slaughter, which, used in collocation with the word *sheep*, convey the idea of sacrifice. This is reinforced in the second simile by the semantic relation to death in the outflowing of the lifeblood. Coincidental with the appearance of these similes, the language starts to become repetitive. The most notable repetition is that of the word *dwindled*, which occurs three times in the one stanza and is repeated in the last. It is also a verb that is marked out from most of the others by its semantic fullness. Apart from this single word, in the last five stanzas Wordsworth has the shepherd use a sort of refrain or burden. This is varied between the lines:

For me it was a woeful day,

which, the first time it appears, is virtually a repetition of an earlier line in the same stanza:

A woeful time it was for me,

and:

My flock, it seemed to melt away,

which echoes the first simile:

To see it melt like snow away!

The amount of repetition is slight when compared with some of the other ballads but in the context of the selection of language in this poem it appears more prominent. With the variations that Wordsworth skilfully employs among the lines, it re-enacts the tragedy without allowing it to become in any sense ludicrous. By altering the placing and wording slightly and keeping it to a bare minimum, Wordsworth uses repetition here to keep the reader from being lulled into false expectations and thereby succeeds in reinforcing the dignity of the shepherd. One is never quite sure at what point the tragedy will be thrust forward. In the final brief and completely unembellished statement, which is not a repetition, it makes its most powerful impact, largely through the quiet understatement:

It is the last of all my flock.

In marked contrast to the effect that Wordsworth achieves through the language given to the shepherd in 'The Last of the Flock' is his use of language in 'The Thorn'. Here, the narrator, who is just occasionally interrupted by the listener/poet, is not telling his own story at all but is a deliberately chosen *persona*. In 'The Advertisement' to the 1798 edition of *Lyrical Ballads* Wordsworth described him simply as a 'loquacious narrator'. However, following criticism of the poem, he expanded his comment in the Note of 1800. It is often stated categorically that Wordsworth says the speaker is actually a 'retired sea captain'. Wordsworth said that this was only an example of the kind of person he had in mind. It is important, however, to read carefully what he says about this kind of man's thinking. It is clear from the language put into his mouth that he is, as Wordsworth originally said, 'garrulous'. Lines such as:

I cannot tell; I wish I could;

and:

No more I know, I wish I did,
And I would tell it all to you;

are sufficient evidence of laboured speech, and also show Wordsworth treading the tightrope of what is effective and what may easily become banal. At times he may appear to slip, as in the much ridiculed description of the pond:

I've measured it from side to side:
'Tis three feet long, and two feet wide.

Advisedly, Wordsworth deleted this from the version of 1820 after Coleridge's criticism of the couplet in *Biographia Literaria* (*BL*, XVII, p. 194). He continued, however, to insist that his original version was the better one and that readers 'ought to like it'.[12]

One of the first questions to come to mind is why Wordsworth chose to use such a narrator at all. It is the only one of these experimental ballads in which he uses a distinct *persona*. Wordsworth gives an indication of his reasons in the Note of 1800 and it is in line with his explorations into the states of mind of certain types of ordinary people. He says:

> it appeared to me proper to select a character like this to exhibit some of the general laws by which superstition acts upon the mind.   (*LB*, p. 288)

We must assume, therefore, that the dramatic *persona* of the narrator and the superstition are of as much importance as Martha Ray. Wordsworth's aims in 'The Thorn' were extremely complex. This hypothesis is made clearer when he says in the 1800 Note that one of his objects in writing the poem was:

> while [he] adhered to the style in which such persons describe, to take care that words, which in their minds are impregnated with passion, should likewise convey passion to Readers who are not accustomed to sympathize with men feeling in that manner of using such language.   (*LB*, p. 288)[13]

'The Thorn' was essentially an experiment in language as much as, if not more than, an account of the tragedy of a deserted, unmarried mother. Wordsworth was deliberately seeking to find how far he could convey to his readers the sensibility and psychological make up of a dramatic speaker by means of a particular way of using language.

One of the features of the language of the narrator in 'The Thorn' is his frequent use of simile. The similes themselves are unlike most of those found in the other narrative ballads. Whereas these are generally concrete and often commonplace, those of 'The Thorn' are often imaginative and suggest ideas to the reader's mind. The likening of the colourful plants growing on the 'hill of moss' to a lady's tapestry has already been noted. The constant description of the hill as 'like an infant's grave in size' and the repeated reference to the height of the thorn as 'Not higher than a two-years' child' and 'Just half a foot in height' (although this last is not a simile) arouse the suspicions of the reader. There is a similar use of metaphor, although not of the obvious kind, in:

Up from the earth these mosses creep,
And this poor thorn they clasp it round
So close, you'd say that they were bent
With plain and manifest intent,
To drag it to the ground.

Here the verbs *clasp* and *creep* are metaphorical and the enduing of these plants with the will to act upon the thorn is a type of pathetic fallacy. The very words, especially adjectives, which are used rather more frequently in this poem than in most of the other narrative ballads, are themselves part of the way in which the atmosphere is built up and are part of the figurative language. *Melancholy* in 'melancholy crop' and *poor* in 'this poor thorn', although not particularly striking as epithets, add to the sense of the impending tragedy that the narrator is producing in the mind of his hearer. These characteristics of the language are also in accord with another part of Wordsworth's Note:

Superstitious men are almost always men of slow faculties and deep feelings; their minds are not loose, but adhesive; they have a reasonable share of imagination, by which word I mean the faculty which produces impressive effects out of simple elements. (*LB*, p. 288)

The rest of this passage accounts for the way in which Wordsworth makes his narrator repeat these and other aspects of his language, rather than introduce new and varied images and descriptions. Wordsworth continues his account of 'super-stitious men':

but they are utterly destitute of fancy, the power by which pleasure and surprize are excited by sudden varieties of situation and by accumulated imagery. (*LB*, p. 288)

Repetition is, therefore, as might be expected, the chief way in which Wordsworth marks the language of his narrator. The most frequently repeated words are those denoting the natural objects associated with the tale: the thorn, the pond, and the 'hill of moss'. These are set against the larger aspects of the landscape within which the events take place, most notably the mountain which Martha Ray frequents, and also the elements of wind, storm and rain. These in turn are placed in their cosmic setting, symbolised by the stars and the sky. We saw this wider setting just lightly touched on in 'The Idiot Boy'. All these words, as well as near synonyms, are repeated time and again. There are in addition clustered repetitions of words. One of these, already noted, is the word *baby*, which can allegedly be seen in the pond. Another example appears in the description of the 'hill of moss':

> All lovely colours there you see,
> All colours that were ever seen.

Repetition of sentences and syntactical structures is similar to that in the other ballads and is easily picked out by the reader. The listener, in his interruptions, which consist mainly of questions, frequently repeats the statements of the narrator in interrogative form. The narrator says:

> And there beside the thorn she sits
> When the blue day-light's in the skies,
> And when the whirlwind's on the hill,
> Or frosty air is keen and still;
> And to herself she cries,

and the listener asks in the following stanza:

> And why sits she beside the thorn
> When the blue day-light's in the sky,
> Or when the whirlwind's on the hill,
> Or frosty air is keen and still,
> And wherefore does she cry? –.

Most obvious is the repetition of the woman's cry itself, which becomes almost a refrain and emphasises the lamentation and the tragedy:

> Oh misery! oh misery!
> O woe is me! oh! misery!

This is the stylised 'miserere' motif found in traditional ballads.

Repetition is naturally linked to tautology. One type of tautology that is not quite the same as the repetitions already mentioned is:

> But that she goes to this old thorn,
> The thorn which I've described to you . . .

The second line, in which the narrator is making sure his point is understood, is the type of laboured and unnecessary explanation that might be expected of such a speaker. The reader, as well as the listener in the poem, knows perfectly well which thorn is being referred to and it is exactly at points like these that Wordsworth runs the risk of losing our sympathy. However, by this time we are far enough into the story to feel an impatience which can create a sense of suspense and urgency. It might be expected that here the listener would interrupt the narrator. Instead the reader is mentally inclined to say, 'Yes, yes, I know; do get on.' Wordsworth thereby creates a tension between the laborious narration and the sense of urgency in the tale itself. He mentions this conflict of differing speeds in the Note of 1800, quoted above (p. 23).

Wordsworth relates the differing speeds to metre. In 'The Thorn' he uses an eleven line stanza – rhyming abcbd eff egg. Apart from the second b and e lines, each of which has three stresses, the stanzas are made up of octosyllabics. The shorter lines almost invariably close a sentence or clause, and also tend to restate, often by means of expansion, what the narrator has already said. Thus they give a sense of matter of factness and finality to the statement, rather than a feeling of something left unsaid or understated, as in 'The Last of the Flock'. We saw an instance of this earlier in the initial description of the thorn:

> It is a mass of knotted joints,
> A wretched thing forlorn.

Here Wordsworth places the three-stress line in apposition to
the preceding nominal group. There is, too, an inversion of the
natural word order, so that the final word also postmodifies the
noun it follows. This has the effect of further rounding off the
statement by producing a falling cadence in the line. The
movement of the short line is perhaps even more obvious in
the following:

> And she is known to every star,
> And every wind that blows.

The first impression here may be that the second line is a
separate clause because of the final verb, a part of speech
found frequently at the end of these short lines. The brief
clause 'that blows', however, is not free-standing but is simply a
postmodification of *wind* and is part of the nominal group of
the prepositional complement following the preposition *to*,
although this has to be inferred from the preceding line. It is in
effect another instance of apparent tautology, since all winds
must blow by definition. It is more the sound of the
postmodifying clause, however, that is important here, allowing
as it does a falling away from the head of the nominal group
wind, while itself finishing on the lexically full word *blows*.

One odd stanza should be noted. This is Stanza XII, which
has three instead of two three-stress lines. The extra one, which
is the sixth line of the stanza, occurs at the turning point in the
tale of Martha Ray, since from the information it conveys stems
all the ensuing and foreseen tragedy:

> And they had fix'd the wedding-day,
> The morning that must wed them both;
> But Stephen to another maid
> Had sworn another oath.
> And with this other maid to church
> *Unthinking Stephen went* –
> Poor Martha! on that woful day
> A cruel, cruel fire, they say,
> Into her bones was sent.   [My italics]

As often with an important point, the variation occurs almost halfway through the poem. The first two lines again exemplify tautology, simply repeating the same statement. Here, too, it takes the form of a clause in apposition to the final nominal group of the preceding line.

A final observation may be made concerning the apparent rambling and repetitious garrulity of the narrator. Not only does Wordsworth adapt it to lengthen his tale and at the same time to create suspense with the slow unfolding of the tragedy: the very repetitions create a cohesiveness that prevents the ballad, which is one of the longest of its kind, from disintegrating. There is a constant tension between the rambling effect of the narrative and the sense of something tight-knit and interwoven. The verbal patterns are constantly interlinked by repetition and near repetition so that the various strands of the tale reverberate forwards and backwards as the narrative progresses.

3 Poems in Ballad Measure

Whilst writing the poems examined in the last chapter, Wordsworth was composing other, shorter poems, often of a more lyrical kind, in strict ballad measure: that is four-lined stanzas of alternating four and three stresses, usually rhyming abab. These include 'We Are Seven', 'Anecdote for Fathers', the pair of poems, 'Expostulation and Reply' and 'The Tables Turned', and the groups known as the 'Matthew' and the 'Lucy' poems. On a first reading, the language seems little different from that of the experimental-type narrative ballads. On closer inspection, one finds that it is slightly less restricted, at least in vocabulary, and the distribution of syntactical features is different. The use of figurative language seems much the same and on the surface, perhaps, there appear to be fewer figures of speech or a slighter use of the same ones: simile, apostrophe and exclamation chiefly. Yet it is in this area that the greatest difference in the language occurs.

The vocabulary of these poems is basically the same as that of the narrative ballads but there are a few more disyllabic words and an occasional one of three syllables. There are more abstract words, especially nouns, and some of these, such as *wisdom*; *lustre*; *strife*; *impulse*, and *intellect*, from 'The Tables Turned' are, perhaps, less commonly used in everyday life, although not notable for any particular poetical quality. The typical Wordsworthian abstract nouns *motion*; *passion*, and *power* appear in these poems. More words of Latin or Romance origin, usually adjectives, occur: *intermitted* in 'intermitted talk', *diurnal* in 'earth's diurnal course', *spontaneous* in 'spontaneous wisdom', *insensate* in 'insensate things', and *vernal* in 'vernal wood'. Verb forms follow a similar pattern, including more of Romance origin, both in their finite forms: *receive*; *review*;

47

confine; and also in the past participles, which may be adjectival: *reclined* and *approved*. None of these words is particularly unusual. The more strikingly literary words are occasional ones of Old English derivation, such as *lore* and *boon*, which may well be used as the result of the ballad revival. The slight difference in vocabulary, therefore, can hardly account for the different and more speculative feeling engendered by these poems.

In syntax short clauses, occupying a single line, are the norm. Where a clause occupies more than one line, the second is frequently of the same pattern as that found in the narrative ballads with a nominal group in apposition to one preceding, as in 'The Fountain':

> And thus the dear old man replied,
> The gray-haired man of glee.

In the clauses occupying more than one line there are more run-on lines. One example where each line of the stanza is run on occurs again in 'The Fountain':

> Now, Matthew! let us try to match
> This water's pleasant tune
> With some old Border-song, or catch
> That suits a summer's noon.

This shows another of the ways in which clauses are lengthened: that is by a restrictive clause, 'That suits a summer's noon', postmodifying a preceding nominal group, in this case the single noun *catch* – a pattern also found in the narrative ballads. In spite of stretching over the whole four lines of the stanza, the structure of this sentence is very simple, with only an expansion of the noun in the final line.

On the whole there is less use of co-ordinate clauses and much less than that which occurred in, say, 'The Idiot Boy'. One might expect a correspondingly greater use of subordination. Although there is some, it is no greater than that used in most of the narrative ballads. There are a very great number of one line clauses, frequently linked paratactically, that is without any conjunction, to the one in the following line. Here is an example:

I have a Boy of five years old;
His face is fair and fresh to see;
His limbs are cast in beauty's mould,
And dearly he loves me.

The influence of Percy's *Reliques* is clear in the third line here.
In 'The Children in the Wood', the ballad to which Wordsworth
repeatedly refers, the words 'And fram'd in beautyes molde'
occur in the description of one of the children. Wordsworth's
version comes in the first stanza of 'Anecdote for Fathers'.
Subordination does occur, as in the following:

I heard a thousand blended notes,
While in a grove I sate reclined,
In that sweet mood when pleasant thoughts
Bring sad thoughts to the mind.

This is slightly more complex but even this is the exception
rather than the rule in these short ballad-type poems. Indeed,
a feature of the clauses is ellipsis rather than lengthening or
expansion, and in this they differ from those in the narrative
ballads. The best-known examples come from the second stanza
of another of the 'Lucy' poems:

A Violet by a mossy stone
   Half-hidden from the eye!
– Fair as a star, when only one
   Is shining in the sky.

Here, the first two lines, punctuated as a sentence, are simply a
nominal group. The second two lines omit the subject and verb
from the head clause: 'She is fair as a star', unless one interprets
'Fair as a star' as an adjectival phrase, a phrase being itself a
contracted and potential clause.[1] The elements of the clauses
are as simple as, if not more simple than, those of the narrative
ballads. Rarely does the head of a nominal group have more
than one premodifier, apart from a determiner, such as *the*;
this; *my*. Even more frequently, there are no premodifiers at all.
This means that there are relatively few adjectives in these
poems. The postmodifiers, if present, are often restrictive

relative clauses, as we have seen. A number of postmodifying prepositional phrases also occurs. An example showing one of each is the following from 'We Are Seven':

> Her hair was thick *with many a curl*
> That clustered round her head.   [My italics]

Like the vocabulary, therefore, the syntax is similar to that of the narrative ballads and where it differs it does not necessarily do so in being more complex. It often appears, superficially at least, less complicated, although it frequently carries greater density or weight of meaning.

The third area with which we were concerned in the narrative ballads was rhetorical and figurative language. In these short poems there are occasional similes, as in:

> Poor Matthew, all his frolics o'er,
> Is silent as a standing pool;

but they are even more sporadic. This is balanced by a slightly greater incidence of metaphor, as in 'this little wreck of fame' from the same poem. The most famous, from the 'Lucy' poems, has already been quoted: 'A Violet by a mossy stone'. Again there is some use of apostrophe and exclamation, but this, too, is less frequent than in the narrative ballads. One figurative use that did not occur in the narrative pieces is personification. This is usually a personification of Nature:

> If Nature, for a favorite Child
> In thee hath tempered so her clay,

which is taken from the same 'Matthew' poem as the two examples of simile and metaphor. Another example of personification, a rather rarer one, is found in 'The Tables Turned':

> The sun, above the mountain's head,
> A freshening lustre mellow
> Through all the long green fields has spread,
> His first sweet evening yellow.

The same 'Matthew' poem also includes examples of apostrophe:

> – Thou soul of god's best earthly mould!
> Thou happy soul!

The fact that so many types of figures of speech occur in 'The Tables Turned' shows that in some of the poems at least there is a fair degree of figurative language, although it is not obtrusive. Other poems, such as 'We Are Seven' and to a lesser extent 'Anecdote for Fathers' have virtually no figurative language at all.

Another poem that seems to avoid figurative language as such is 'The Fountain'. In one stanza from it:

> Thus fares it still in our decay:
> And yet the wiser mind
> Mourns less for what age takes away
> Than what it leaves behind,

the language seems little different from that of the narrative ballads. It is almost wholly monosyllabic and, apart from the abstract nouns *decay* and *age*, the vocabulary is of Germanic origin. The language is slightly less concrete, and the verb *fares* is one of those words from the basic native stock that draws attention to itself because it is a slightly archaic word, which accounts for its slightly literary sound. Generally, however, the vocabulary is so simple that the reader can easily miss the degree of complexity in the syntax of the second clause, with its two embedded correlative clauses, 'less ... than ...', in the adverbial element that occurs after the verb *mourns*. Here the almost colloquial verbs, *takes away* and *leaves behind*, deflect the mind from the more complex syntax and the meaning that it embodies. These three lines, however, afford the clue to the main linguistic difference between the narrative ballads and the poems we are now considering. This difference runs across all three strands of vocabulary, grammar and figurative language, and is itself a form of metaphor. At first sight there may seem to be no metaphor in the sense in which we generally think of it, but once it is pointed out it is fairly easy to see that the verbs associated with the abstract noun *age* are in fact metaphorical. *Age*, being abstract, cannot literally either take anything away or leave anything behind. These are dynamic verbs, the action denoted only capable of being performed by animate and, usually, since they frequently include a degree of intention, human agents. We are, however, so used to using these verbs in this way that their figurative import is overlooked. The usage has become part of the 'system' of the language and we are apt not to notice it unless attention is drawn to it.

These short poems in ballad measure abound in this type of metaphor. Often it is located wholly in the verbs, as in this example from the same poem:

> Down to the vale this water steers,
> How merrily it goes!
> 'Twill murmur on a thousand years,
> And flow as now it flows.

The verb *steers* is a transitive verb but here it is used intransitively and with an inanimate subject. The metaphorical nature of this usage is fairly easy to detect, since water cannot normally steer itself or anything else. The verb is restricted in its literal, non-figurative sense to human agents and generally refers to the guiding of craft, in Wordsworth's time usually water-craft. In its use here it is not part of the system of the language and is therefore more easily identified as a metaphor. The second verb attached to the subject *water* is *murmur*. Although this is less obviously metaphorical, partly because of its onomatopoeic quality, strictly it is a metaphor. It was originally restricted to animate agents but because of its sound it has long been transferred to certain inanimate objects, especially wind and water. It has become the normal, unmarked way of speaking of the sound of flowing water. The metaphors in these lines do not end with the verbs. The adverb *merrily* is also metaphorical, since an inanimate object cannot be either merry or sad.

Although 'Anecdote for Fathers' seems to be without any metaphor, a verbal metaphor does occur in:

> Then did the boy his tongue unlock.

Here the verb and complement, *tongue unlock*, could be replaced by the single verb 'speak'. Metaphor means the transference of words from one sense to another. Frequently, this involves using a concrete word in an abstract sense or a material process to express a mental one. Metaphorical language of this type is not, however, confined to vocabulary. It can extend beyond single words to the syntax of the whole sentence and is more accurately described in these cases as 'grammatical' metaphor.[2]

It is not always possible, as it is in the example from 'Anecdote for Fathers', to replace the metaphorical element with a single word or even a phrase. The whole structure of the clause has to be reworked if one wishes to express the meaning in a literal way. In the earlier example:

His limbs were cast in beauty's mould,

it is easy to see that the metaphor runs through the whole clause. We uncovered the metaphors in the first stanza from 'The Fountain' and related them to the word *age* and the verbs of which it was the subject, but a closer scrutiny will reveal that here also the metaphor extends through the entire three lines of the second clause. If we try to paraphrase this clause literally, we might have something like 'If a person is wise he will not mourn for what has been taken from him as he has grown older but for what he has been left with'. This attempt at 'unscrambling' the metaphor results in the idea that one should mourn for what one continues to possess and, on the surface, appears nonsensical. A literal rewording, it seems, still leaves us at a remove from the true meaning. However, one must ask what it is that 'age leaves behind'? Surely, it is memories. These memories are what remain and what are to be lamented for the pain they bring. The literal paraphrase is, in this sense, correct. That this is almost certainly the right interpretation is clear in the context of the whole poem. Matthew remembers with sadness his former vigour. Later it becomes apparent that he also grieves over his children, who have died. The stanzas immediately following the one we have been looking at reinforce the correctness of this reading:

The Blackbird in the summer trees,

The Lark upon the hill,
Let loose their carols when they please,
Are quiet when they will.

With Nature never do *they* wage
A foolish strife; they see
A happy youth, and their old age
Is beautiful and free.

The birds have no memories to disturb their acceptance of life. It will be immediately apparent that these stanzas, too, contain much grammatical metaphor, although it is less complex and less dense. Indeed, metaphor is everywhere in the poem.

It is this use of grammatical metaphor that distinguishes the language of these short poems in ballad metre from the experimental and narrative ballads. Even here, however, usage is not consistent, and these poems can be grouped by the amount of metaphor they contain as well as by subject matter. It is not perhaps surprising that the two frequently coincide.

Although many grammatical metaphors can be recognised most easily from the verb, it is frequently the presence of an abstract noun that alerts us to the fact that we are entering the metaphorical mode of expression. For example, we can say: 'Mary smelled the new bread baking as she entered the door'. This is literal. However, the sentence can be recast so that the verb *smell* becomes an abstract noun: 'As she entered the door, Mary was aware of the smell of new bread baking.' The noun *smell* is the complement of the verb *to be aware of*. As such it is what is called a 'participant' in the structure of the sentence and is metaphorical. As a nominalised complement it can function as the subject if the sentence is again reworded. This can be done in a number of ways, all of which are clearly metaphorical:

The smell of new bread baking greeted Mary as she entered the door.
The smell of new bread baking assailed Mary's nostrils.
The smell of new bread baking floated out of the house.

The abstract noun, in this case formed from a verb, does not have to be a subject or complement to be metaphorical. It can be the complement of a prepositional phrase, as in the following, where the noun is not formed from a verb: 'John spoke to Mary with anger in his voice'. This could be rewritten as 'the anger in John's voice struck Mary when he spoke to her', or 'battered Mary's ears' or 'rained down on Mary's head'.

The fact that Wordsworth's poetry is full of this kind of metaphor has been noted before. J. P. Ward says that his 'writing pulls in metaphors very much as he goes, simply because the nominals teem'.[3] Another readily identified example of a grammatical metaphor is 'A wonderful sight met Mary's eyes', which is derived from the literal, 'Mary saw something wonderful'. The nouns do not necessarily have to be abstract. An example of a concrete noun as subject is 'The fifth day saw the mountaineers at the summit'.[4] Wordsworth has a very similar example to this in the second line of the following quotation from 'The Thorn':

And they had fix'd the wedding day,
The morning that must wed them both.

There are other types of grammatical metaphor but this is Wordsworth's basic type.

I have said that the short poems in ballad measure differ from the narrative ballads in that they make use of this type of metaphor but have quoted as the first example of Wordsworth's use one from 'The Thorn'. This must be followed up. It is a characteristic of all normal speech and discourse that it contains this kind of grammatical metaphor. The amount varies according to the type of discourse and the register but none is wholly without it. Only the speech of very young children seems not to use it and also children's traditional songs and nursery rhymes. It has been suggested that these have survived as children's rhymes for this very reason.[5] Nursery rhymes frequently originated as topical or satirical rhymes and although frequently containing fantastic expressions are almost always literal and incapable of any more literal substitution. They can often be taken symbolically, and originally they probably were, but they can also be understood in a quite literal way and this may account for their appeal to young children. From this we might expect that many traditional ballads would also contain little or no grammatical metaphor but this does not seem always to be the case. However, certain of the ballads in Percy's *Reliques*, such as 'The Cruelty of Barbara Allen' and 'The Children in the Wood' do not include very much of this type of metaphor and what there is seems to be extremely idiomatic, even formulaic, or appears rather superficial, as if added for the sake of embellishment. This is very much the pattern of this type of metaphor as Wordsworth uses it occasionally in his narrative ballads. Odd examples such as the one from 'The Thorn' can be found, most of them either easily passsed over, since they have become, as this one, a normal mode of expression, or else rather striking because instead of being built into the syntax and increasing the semantic complexity of the poet's statement, they are superficial, adding little to the meaning. They may add to something else as we can see from the lines already quoted from 'The Thorn':

And she is known to every star
And every wind that blows.

There is an undoubted heightening of the poetical quality here but it is at first difficult to locate. The words are as simple as any in the ballads and the metaphor is not immediately obvious. However, it is almost certainly the use of the metaphor that accounts for the heightening. There are a number of grammatical metaphors in 'The Last of the Flock'. Again, this may convey the emotional state of the shepherd, who is telling his own tragedy. One example is of the kind seen already:

And every year increased my store.

There is the repeated use of the verb *melt* to describe the diminishing flock, and a related example in:

It was a vein that never stopp'd –
Like blood-drops from my heart they dropp'd.

Here, the metaphor of the first line is combined with a simile and this is often the case in the narrative ballads. The combination seems to point to the fact that the metaphors are more on the surface and less deeply embedded in the whole expression. Otherwise they are of the other type mentioned earlier: expressions that have become a normal part of the language system and are therefore essentially idiomatic.

It is the semantic complexities that are expressed metaphorically. Many of these consist of well-known and often-quoted lines, which people frequently do not even realise they do not understand. Hazlitt noted this very early. In 1825 he wrote:

> Hence the unaccountable mixture of seeming simplicity and real abstruseness in the *Lyrical Ballads*. Fools have laughed at, wise men scarcely understood them.[6]

Much later, Helen Darbishire has said, 'Wordsworth's poetry is steeped in these images, and his words carry them so naturally that we hardly notice them.'[7] It is not without significance that such lines are often memorable; this may be because they contain a poetic quality that is elusive. One example less difficult to understand than many is:

> And 'tis my faith that every flower
> Enjoys the air it breathes.

As is often the case when we think Wordsworth is being metaphorical, he is stating here what to him is a fact. This then is not a true metaphor at all in Wordsworthian expression and thought. Another example, more genuine and also more perplexing, is:

> One impulse from a vernal wood,
> May teach you more of man,
> Of moral evil and of good,
> Than all the sages can.

Whatever Wordsworth meant by *impulse*, a much debated point, it is clear that it cannot *teach* in any literal, concrete or material sense of the word.[8] Another example occurs almost immediately after in the same poem:

> Our meddling intellect
> Misshapes the beauteous forms of things.

This, Wordsworth glosses himself:

> – We murder to dissect.

But what does this mean? We murder in order to dissect things or the dissection of things results in our murdering them? The elliptical syntax makes the meaning ambiguous, although it matters little which way round we look at it, and probably Wordsworth intended both senses. In any case, a moment's reflection tells us that the gloss is itself metaphorical. Wordsworth uses a material process to represent what is clearly intended to be a mental one. There is a linguistic sleight of hand here, for it seems as if a literal interpretation of the meaning is being given.

As in the first example quoted from 'The Thorn', the metaphor frequently escapes the reader because of the apparent simplicity of the vocabulary and syntax, and because the metaphorical expression seems to be the accepted and idiomatic one. By missing the metaphor, however, the semantic complexity itself can be overlooked. This is why some people think that Wordsworth's poetry is simple to the point of absurdity. Another well-known stanza using grammatical metaphor comes in 'Expostulation and Reply':

> Nor less I deem that there are powers
> Which of themselves our minds impress;
> That we can feed this mind of ours
> In a wise passiveness.

The companion poem, 'The Tables Turned', makes the intention of these lines more explicit by combining personification with the metaphor:

> Let Nature be your teacher.
> She has a world of ready wealth,
> Our minds and hearts to bless –

Spontaneous wisdom breathed by health,
Truth breathed by chearfulness.

This sounds simple enough but the meaning is so metaphorically compressed that any attempt to substitute a literal paraphrase results in a tediously long explanation that loses all the
immediate impact of Wordsworth's metaphorical mode of expression.

Wordsworth was himself unusually aware of the metaphorical
nature of language. In the Preface of 1815 he links the faculty
of imagination to 'image', both in its visual sense and in relation
to figures of speech in language (*PW*, III, pp. 30–2). For
instance, he demonstrates the use of the verb *hang* in its literal
sense by referring to a parrot hanging in its cage by its claws or
beak; in its visual sense – partly figurative – from *King Lear*,
when Gloucester and Edgar are discussing the cliffs at Dover:

> Half way down
> Hangs one who gathers samphire . . .   (IV, vi, 15–16)

and finally in its completely metaphorical sense, from Milton's
description in *Paradise Lost* of the appearance of a fleet to which
he compares the flying Fiend:

> As when farr off at Sea a Fleet descri'd
> Hangs in the Clouds . . .   (II, 636–7)

Similarly, he cites his own poem, 'Resolution and Independence',
to illustrate the metaphorical use of certain verbs:

> Over his own sweet voice the Stock-dove *broods*;

and:

> His voice was *buried* among trees,
> Yet to be come at by the breeze.

Let us now examine the use of grammatical metaphor in
relation to the poems as a group. The use is not consistent and
the poems can be subdivided according to the amount of

metaphor they contain as well as by their subject matter. That the two generally coincide may be partly because the dates of composition indicate that Wordsworth thought of them in groups and would be likely to use the same type of language in each group.

The two poems 'We Are Seven' and 'Anecdote for Fathers' both explore the way in which the minds of children work. They contain no, or very little, grammatical metaphor. The example from 'Anecdote for Fathers' quoted earlier, although a good instance for explaining grammatical metaphor, was not used to convey any complicated meaning or idea. The examples that occur in 'We Are Seven' are of the type that are part of English idiom:

> 'Twas throwing words away: for still
> The little Maid would have her will.

These two lines contain two separate grammatical metaphors, the first an idiom, the second, involving the verb *have*, which has not been discussed but often involves a type of grammatical metaphor.[9] However, it does not extend beyond the verb and complement and these could be replaced by the single verb *insist*. It is not surprising that 'We Are Seven' is quite frequently placed for discussion with the longer narrative ballads. It is also worth noting that these two poems were written early in 1798, alongside 'The Idiot Boy', 'The Last of the Flock' and 'Simon Lee'.[10]

On the other hand, 'Expostulation and Reply' and 'The Tables Turned', written just after, at the end of May or beginning of June 1798, both contain much more metaphorical language, which is also closely integrated into the meaning of the poems. The 'Matthew' poems, however, which were composed between October 1798 and the early months of 1799, seem to have less again, although one stanza from 'The Fountain', which shows an extremely dense use of grammatical metaphor, has been examined in detail. The noteworthy point about 'The Fountain' and 'The Two April Mornings', both of which concern the passage of time and consequent bereavement, is that at the crux of each poem Wordsworth reverts to the literal mode of expression. In 'The Fountain', when the narrator impulsively offers to be a son to Matthew in place of his own lost children, the old man replies:

Alas! that cannot be.

Similarly, in 'The Two April Mornings', when Matthew recounts how he saw in the churchyard the girl who reminded him of his own dead daughter, although he describes her in metaphorical terms and with simile, his ultimate reaction is expressed literally:

I looked at her and looked again:
– And did not wish her mine.

Both of these important turning points in a poem include another linguistic feature, frequently found in these shorter poems and hitherto unmentioned. That is the negative expression used to convey the essential part of a poem's meaning. This is most marked in the 'Lucy' poems, which were written about the same time as the 'Matthew' group, possibly slightly earlier. Although there is grammatical metaphor in these, as in:

A Slumber did my spirit seal:

and:

Strange fits of passion I have known,

the semantic complexities of some of the shorter poems are not present, even though they express Wordsworth's philosophy just as fully. The negative element is very strong, especially in the two shorter poems of the group of three included here. The strange isolation of Lucy is emphasised in 'She dwelt among th'untrodden ways', in lines such as:

A Maid whom there were none to praise,
    And very few to love,

and again later:

> She lived unknown, and few could know
>   When Lucy ceased to be.

The circumlocution 'ceased to be', besides itself being more negative than 'she died', is typical of the passive element which in these poems is linked to the negative. 'A Slumber did my spirit seal' is expressed almost wholly by negation, from the oblique negative of the opening line, through the rest of the stanza:

> I had no human fears:
> She seemed a thing that could not feel
>   The touch of earthly years.

Notice that the metaphorical element is still present. These constructions build up to the strong negative statements of:

> No motion has she now, no force
> She neither hears nor sees.

The non-finite clause at the end, which could be taken as a postmodifier of *she*, seems to finish grammatically on a more positive note:

> Rolled round in earth's diurnal course
>   With rocks and stones and trees.

It matches the positively expressed ending of the previous poem:

> But she is in her Grave, and Oh!
>   The difference to me.

The understatement of the final minor or verbless clause of this last line seems to be even more emphatically positive because of its elliptical nature. But the positive grammatical expression of the final lines of both these poems conveys a partially negative meaning. This is especially so in the second. The 'difference' is itself very great but it is a difference which is rooted in something having been taken away or lost, something which is absent. The positive statement of the other poem also emphasises Lucy's complete lack of animation and volition, her utter passivity. Yet, as is clear from all the poems, the passive state is itself a positive thing which leads to the acquisition of wisdom. Negation, therefore, whether grammatical or semantic, can paradoxically imply the opposite. Perhaps this is why the conclusion of both poems is expressed positively. It could be argued, therefore, that in the 'Lucy' poems, by using affirmative statements to convey negative meaning – another kind of transference – Wordsworth has extended metaphor into a new dimension.

One should not stress too much any notion of a chronological development. Apart from the fact that they were all written within the space of one year, Wordsworth was writing very many different kinds of verse at the same time. It is certain that he was experimenting with techniques very intensively. What should be noted is that, while using the same basic vocabulary and syntactic structures as in the narrative ballads, Wordsworth includes in these shorter poems grammatical metaphor, which he virtually excluded, either deliberately or instinctively, from the narrative ballads. It is chiefly by extending the language into metaphor that Wordsworth achieves a breadth of expression and of meaning that completely belies the basic simplicity of the other linguistic features.

4 Blank Verse – Diction

Wordsworth's blank verse can be roughly divided into three types: narrative, descriptive and what may be called contemplative or reflective. No poem is written entirely in one mode and some contain all three. This division is rather different from what we shall find in Coleridge, whose blank verse is basically reflective, although it contains elements of description and even a small amount of narrative. All the poems to be examined were written in fairly close sequence, and one hesitates, therefore, to postulate a progression but there does appear to be some development. Certain features are common to all the blank verse but others vary according to the type, and the variation becomes more distinct in the later poems, 'Michael' showing the greatest differentiation among its various parts. The poems which are most accessible to linguistic analysis are, once again, those in *Lyrical Ballads*. Representative poems are 'Tintern Abbey' (July 1798), mainly reflective; 'The Old Cumberland Beggar' (1800), mainly descriptive; and 'Michael' (1800), which is generally considered to be narrative. 'The Brothers' (also 1800) must also be taken into account, although here the narrative is in the form of dialogue. One of the difficulties of examining Wordsworth's poetry is that, as with the ballads, in this early period he rarely writes the same type of poem twice. Other pieces, mainly fragments, often incorporated later into other poems, also belong to this period and are of interest for comparison.

The features that are common to all the blank verse poetry, including pieces written before the 1798 edition of *Lyrical Ballads*, will be mentioned first. The diction is very much more abstract and literary than that of the ballads, although it still includes a high number of concrete and basic words. The

64

proportion varies slightly in different poems, as does the type. The concrete diction frequently comes, as might be expected, in description of natural objects. 'The Ruined Cottage', which was published in 1814 as Book I of *The Excursion*, was one of Wordsworth's first attempts at composing blank verse. It was virtually completed before 'Tintern Abbey', the first of the blank verse poems to be included in *Lyrical Ballads*, was begun.[1] The descriptions of natural and everyday objects, both those belonging to the world of nature and those referring to domestic life, are more precise and, therefore, contain more particularised vocabulary than some of the later blank verse poems. The following description of part of Margaret's neglected garden is a good example:

> The gooseberry trees that shot in long [lank slips,][2]
> Or currants, hanging from their leafless stems,
> In scanty strings . . .

In this brief but vivid picture of the currants, a present participial clause postmodifies the noun *currants*. This is typical of Wordsworth's later method of progressively expanding the nominal group, but the precision of the adjectives *leafless* and *scanty* in the embedded prepositional phrases that follow contrasts with his use of more general and often abstract types of adjectives. Adjectives such as *sweet* in 'sensations sweet' or *abundant* in 'abundant recompense' or, more concrete but hardly striking, *blue* in 'blue sky', are typical of the blank verse poems written slightly later. Another example from 'The Ruined Cottage' describes sound:

> nor could my weak arm disperse
> The insect host which gathered round my face
> And joined their murmurs to the tedious noise
> Of seeds of bursting gorse which crackled round.

In the third line the nasals and sibilants create the sound of the buzzing insects, while in contrast the various plosive consonants of the final line convey a vivid acoustic image of the bursting seed pods.[3] Later, Wordsworth changed the eighteenth-century sounding 'insect host' to 'host of insects' and omitted the onomatopoeic final two lines, substituting 'And ever with me as I paced along'. One domestic detail in 'The Ruined Cottage', which appeared very early in the draft versions[4] is the following description of how Margaret's husband used to make the cottage weather-proof before the onset of winter:

> for he was gone whose hand,
> At the first nippings of October frost,
> Closed up each chink and with fresh bands of straw
> Chequered the green-grown thatch.

A similar example, which changed in form during the course of composition, is the description of the broken bowl, which Margaret used for fetching water from the well for passing travellers and which is sometimes seen as a symbol of her broken life. It comes when the well is first mentioned:

> A spider's web
> Across its mouth hung to the water's edge,
> And on the wet and slimy foot-stone lay
> The useless fragment of a wooden bowl.

This was later altered to:

> Upon the slimy foot-stone I espied
> The useless fragment of a wooden bowl,
> Green with the moss of years, and subject only
> To the handling of the elements.[5]

Here the concrete description of the spider's web in the first version is omitted. The description of the state of the bowl is typical of the later blank verse poems. It is true that the specificity of *fragment* and *wooden bowl* is further particularised by the addition of *green moss* but this gives way in the final clause to the abstract nouns, *handling* and *elements*, together with the verbal adjective *subject to* with its rather undefined and passive connotations. This revision is important as it shows clearly Wordsworth's tendency to move away from the specific towards the general.

'The Ruined Cottage' marks another development in

Wordsworth's use of diction in his blank verse, since it was in
this poem that he finally abandoned the Gothick type of vocabulary and imagery for a plainer, more matter-of-fact idiom. In
the first version the Pedlar is made to set his reminiscences in a
night scene, typical of Gothick poetry. The description of the
cottage, too, contains all the ingredients of a 'Romantic' Gothick
atmosphere:

> And when the poor mans horse that shelters there
> Turns from the beating wind and open sky
> The iron li[n]ks with which his feet are clogg'd
> Mix their dull clanking with the heavy sound
> Of falling rain a melancholy . . .

Later these lines, never completed, were abandoned along with
the atmosphere of mysterious melancholy.[6] The more everyday
style to which Wordsworth turned, apparently deliberately, was
to form the basis of his language in *Lyrical Ballads* and that of
his later poetry. He himself said in a letter written on 1 April
1843 'no change has taken place in my manner for the last
forty-five years'. (*LY*, IV, 423 [III, 1159]).[7]

Descriptive passages in Wordsworth's poetry most frequently
bring to mind his preoccupation with the world of nature but
the two first quotations from 'The Ruined Cottage' show him
using words related to everyday objects of household living and
rural occupations, and these are well represented in the poems
of *Lyrical Ballads*. Shepherd's crooks, spinning wheels, lanterns,
tableware and similar objects recur and create a sense of
location and solidity which complements the more abstract,
contemplative passages. The following from 'Michael' is typical:

> all
> Turned to their cleanly supper-board, and there,
> Each with his mess of pottage and skimmed milk,
> Sate round their basket piled with oaten cakes,
> And their plain home-made cheese.

The echo of biblical language in 'mess of pottage' should be
noted. Direct use of biblical phrases is relatively rare in
Wordsworth's poetry, although its sound and cadence constantly

reflect the influence of the Bible. This homely scene, depicted solely by means of concrete words, gives substance to the tragedy that follows. Later there will be occasion to note Coleridge's rather different use of homely imagery in such blank verse poems as 'Frost at Midnight' and 'This Lime-Tree Bower My Prison'.

There is a third and perhaps more unexpected set of concrete terms in these poems. They occur more sporadically but are surprising partly because they seem to be singularly unpoetic, certainly not 'Romantic', and far removed from the world of nature we habitually associate with Wordsworth. These are to do with legal and business matters: words such as *mortgage*, *interest*, *estate*, and others appear in certain poems and it is part of Wordsworth's achievement that in the context of a whole poem they do not seem particularly out of place. Naturally, in brief quotations, such as the one below, taken from 'The Brothers', they do seem obtrusive:

> the old man still preserv'd
> A chearful mind, and buffeted with bond,
> Interest and mortgages.

The appearance of words from this legal register is more easily understood when one remembers that Wordsworth often had a social object in view. 'The Old Cumberland Beggar', for example, is directed unequivocally towards the landowners, or 'Statesmen', as Wordsworth calls them, who were seeking to alter the Poor Laws. It should perhaps also be remembered that Wordsworth's uncle, who was one of his guardians after his father died, was a solicitor, and words of this type would have been early assimilated by the boy as a natural part of his vocabulary. They were ready to hand when needed and probably sprang more easily to his mind than they might have done to those of other poets. The use of the word *indentures* in 'The Idiot Boy' has already been mentioned. It is also perhaps not without significance that 'The Children in the Wood', the ballad in Percy's *Reliques*, so admired by Wordsworth, contains a surprisingly high number of legal terms.

The minutely particularised descriptions of natural objects, in the extracts quoted from 'The Ruined Cottage', tend to become generalised in Wordsworth's later poems, even if the language in which they are expressed is relatively simple. The most obvious example of this comes in the ode on 'Intimations of Immortality' (?1802–4):

> – But there's a Tree, of many, one,
> A single Field which I have looked upon.

The individuality is stated but the individual description is missing. This generalisation is very evident in the only blank verse poem in the 1798 edition of *Lyrical Ballads*. In the opening lines of 'Tintern Abbey' we read:

> Once again
> Do I behold these steep and lofty cliffs,
> Which on a wild secluded scene impress
> Thoughts of more deep seclusion; and connect
> The landscape with the quiet of the sky.

In spite of the two concrete words, *cliffs* and *sky*, the description is generalised and abstract with the words *scene* and *landscape* fitting in with the other abstract vocabulary, which is used to convey a mood rather than any concrete and visually clear image of a specific scene. The vegetation and other details of this broadly depicted landscape are nevertheless frequently denoted by basic concrete words, usually of native stock:

> These hedge-rows, hardly hedge-rows, little lines
> Of sportive wood run wild.

Even here, however, the minute particularity of the quotations from 'The Ruined Cottage' is lacking and the scene conveyed remains impressionistic, perhaps because it veers away from the strictly literal towards the figurative and metaphorical. The setting is a springboard for Wordsworth's thoughts rather than something to be described for its own sake. It is, however, puzzling that Wordsworth very often conveys a more abstract impression than the concreteness of the words he uses would seem to suggest. Part of the answer to this lies in the non-specific or more general type of concrete word that he frequently chooses.

A brief word here about specific and generic terms may be useful. *Oak* and *ash* are specific terms in relation to the generic word *tree*, which embraces them both, as well as all the other specific names of trees. *Tree* is itself specific on the level of *flower*; *shrub*; *bush*; *grass* and all other words which are covered by the generic term *vegetation*. On the other hand, *tool*; *utensil* or *implement* (a favourite Wordsworthian word) are generic in relation to *scythe*; *spindle*; *crook* and so on. In the later blank verse, Wordsworth tends to use the more generic words in preference to the more specific in many cases, although both may be concrete. There is another group of words for which Wordsworth seems to have a predilection. These are words like *rock*. *Rock* is generic, having, to all intents and purposes, no set of specific words into which it can be further sub-classified.[8] It can only be made specific by an expansion of the noun itself by pre- or postmodification, as, for example, 'the large, menacing grey rock, fissured with many cracks'. Many words fall into this group, in which we may include the type such as *sky* or *sun*, for which there is only one referent. The preciseness of a word like *currants*, therefore, which was further specified by the descriptive adjectives and nouns, becomes general and imprecise. These general words often slide into completely abstract terms. It must, however, be stressed that Wordsworth's use of these more general or generic words does not mean that he did not have a particular object in mind. It is merely that he tended to *describe* that object less. Frequently, as in 'Tintern Abbey', he was thinking of one very specific object or scene.

There is a semblance of specificity in the lines immediately following the opening ones quoted above:

> I again repose
> Here, under this dark sycamore, and view
> These plots of cottage-ground, these orchard-tufts,
> Which, at this season, with their unripe fruits,
> Among the woods and copses lose themselves,
> Nor, with their green and simple hue, disturb
> The wild green landscape.

Wordsworth uses a number of definite articles or specific determiners: *the* and *these*. He is lying under one particular tree, the species of which is designated by the word *sycamore*, but the orchard trees are more general in that they are simply fruit trees. The other trees mentioned are further generalised in the phrase 'woods and copses', and finally all are integrated into the completely abstract word *landscape*. There is some return to more particular detail in the description of the hedgerows in the lines that follow, but thereafter the scene becomes again generalised. This is achieved by the use of plural nouns and also through the indefinite and impersonal pronoun *some* used of the hermit:

> these pastoral farms
> Green to the very door; and wreathes of smoke
> Sent up, in silence, from among the trees,
> With some uncertain notice, as might seem,
> Of vagrant dwellers in the houseless woods,
> Or of some hermit's cave, where by his fire
> The hermit sits alone.

This is no particular hermit (the representative *the* is used in the second reference to him) and, indeed, the uncertainty as to whether the smoke comes from his cave or from 'vagrant dwellers' also works against any idea of the specific. The lack of a sense of definition is further enhanced by the negative derivatives, *uncertain* and *houseless*, and the interposed interpersonal clause expressing a possibility rather than a certainty: 'as might seem'.[9] The very loose wording of this entire line reinforces the vagueness of the word *seem*. This is a frequent word in Wordsworth's verse and emphasises his lack of dogmatism, and reticence about ultimate realities.

At the beginning of the next section the entire landscape dissolves into abstraction: 'These forms of beauty'. The two nouns used here are commonplace, but abstract, and they convey an entirely abstract idea of the physically present scene that the poet/narrator is contemplating. This use of relatively simple and ordinary words in combination to express highly abstract concepts is another part of the answer to the question: how does Wordsworth give the impression of abstractness when using everyday, and even concrete, vocabulary?[10] When further on in 'Tintern Abbey' the natural objects are once more recalled, the words used are representative rather than denoting specific objects, and this is another way in which Wordsworth achieves an abstract effect. The words themselves are commonplace and basic enough (an elevated but typically Wordsworthian word *cataract* occurs but only one): *hills*; *mountains*; *streams*; *woods*; *rivers*; *meadows*, and so on. The fact that these are usually referred to in the plural reinforces the fact that they are not particularised. Furthermore, they rarely have any premodifying adjectives and where they do these are unexceptional: '*tall* rock'; '*blue* sky'; '*deep and gloomy* wood'. These are very different from the type of adjective used in the quotation from 'The Ruined Cottage' describing the currants. Adjectives in the blank verse, as in the ballads, play a relatively small part, although occasionally they are very striking.

The move from the particular to the general itself raises a further question: why should Wordsworth wish to do this? In a poem such as 'Tintern Abbey', which is centred on a deeply felt personal experience, it is partly because Wordsworth attempts not merely to describe or record his own experience but to enable the reader to feel the same mood of exaltation and the sense of 'something far more deeply interfused' from those natural objects which happen to be part of his, the reader's, experience. Wordsworth is recreating his experience for himself – hence the specific; and, at the same time, projecting it for readers to share the same sensations through their own experiences of a similar kind. Wordsworth, therefore, seeks to help the reader to call upon these different experiences by moving towards the general.

There is another point here, however, that must be taken into account and that is the historical dimension of poetry. The late eighteenth century was not concerned with the particular or individual but with what was common to all men and affected people equally. As late as 1807 we find Wordsworth writing to Lady Beaumont:

> There is scarcely one of my Poems which does not aim to direct the attention to some moral sentiment, or to some general principle, or law of thought, or of our intellectual constitution.   (*MY*, I, 148 [I, 128])

Here Wordsworth stresses both the generality which is inherent in the particular and the fact that he has tried to show this in his poetry. That he believed this was the function of poetry is not in doubt. When Wordsworth speaks of *affections* and *passions* in 'Tintern Abbey' he indicates that his intention was to rouse in others the emotions he experienced himself.

An example of how Wordsworth can maintain a balance between the general and the specific occurs at the beginning of Book VIII of *The Prelude*. Returning from London to his native Lakes, the poet sees a rural fair, which is small enough in comparison with the metropolis, 'a little Family of Men, / Twice twenty with their Children and their Wives,' for everyone to be an individual, known and recognised annually as the fair day comes round. The description of the pedlar woman runs:

> hither, too,
> From far, with Basket, slung upon her arm,
> Of Hawker's Wares, books, pictures, combs, and pins,
> Some aged Woman finds her way again,
> Year after year a punctual visitant!   (VIII, 27–31)

The individual aspect lies in the detail with which her wares are named and in the final line, especially the phrase 'Year after year' and the word *punctual*. The generality occurs in the word *Some*. Although an individual, she is not any particular woman. The traders at the village fair are unknown to the poet and hence have no specific identity for him or for the readers. Indeed, they are probably not even known by name to the local people, although they recognise the woman from her yearly appearance. She is not part of the local community for she comes 'From far', but is still a *known individual*. Here, Wordsworth uses the general aspect for a rather different purpose from that outlined above.

This brings us to another area of his vocabulary, which occurs in *The Prelude*, and there only in Book VII 'Residence in London'. Wordsworth is not generally associated with town life and its relevant vocabulary but in this book he is wholly intent on evoking the spirit of the city. In contrast to the little domestic fair he draws a faceless, anonymous picture. Because this area of Wordsworth's vocabulary is so different from that which he normally uses it is the more noteworthy. The description of London begins with a plentiful use of proper names: St Paul's; Westminster; the Guildhall; the pleasure gardens of Vauxhall and Ranelagh and others. These, however, although appearing specific are all place names and serve merely to give a framework to the life of the capital:

> the quick dance
> Of colours, lights and forms, the Babel din,
> The endless stream of men, and moving things, . . .
> The wealth, the bustle and the eagerness,
> The glittering Chariots with their pamper'd Steeds,
> Stalls, Barrows, Porters.   (VII, 156–63)

The vocabulary moves from impressionistic abstract words: *colours, lights and forms* (reminiscent of a stanza we examined in 'The Idiot Boy') to abstractions mixing various attributes and attitudes. Finally concrete words are used, as if a confused picture were gradually coming into focus. After a brief detailed description Wordsworth returns to generalities while still keeping to a largely concrete vocabulary:

> Here there and everywhere a weary Throng
> The Comers and the Goers face to face,
> Face after face; the string of dazzling Wares,
> Shop after shop . . .   (VII, 171–4)

This alternation continues as he runs swiftly through the whole gamut of city life: the cosmopolitan nature of the population (here again proper names are used but the Jew, Turk, Italian and so on are merely representative figures); typical street dwellers; vagrants; entertainers; museums 'of wild Beasts' (a feature of the time); theatres; the Law courts; even the back streets: 'Private Courts / Gloomy as Coffins.' This last brief quotation if written in prose would surely be identified with Dickens and is evocative in exactly the same way as his descriptions of London. It is noteworthy that there are more adjectives in this Book and more attempt at vivid description than in the parts dealing with the natural landscape. Interiors, too, are clearly observed and very different from the normal rural cottage rooms:

> the lustres, lights,
> The carving and the gilding, paint and glare,
> And all the mean upholstery of the place.   (VII, 440–2)

Specific, concrete details like *upholstery* are mingled with emotive abstractions, such as *glare* to create a picture far removed from the natural world. The 'upholstery' itself is premodified by the adjective *mean*, indicating a stale shabbiness in contrast to the freshness of the country. There is an abundance of concrete nouns denoting buildings, occupations and other sights found in the city. The adjectives are vastly different from those in the nature passages, as the quotations show: words such as *glittering*; *dazzling*; *crude*; *greedy*; *mean* and *suburban* – all intended to be pejorative. Wordsworth also includes a number of similes and even metaphors. These, rather surprisingly, are quite often drawn from rural life, perhaps to emphasise the contrast with the city. One of the most memorable is of the child he sees with its mother in a theatre:

> He was in limbs, in face a cottage rose
> Just three parts blown.   (VII, 379–80)

Perhaps also to draw attention to the continual movement and unrest in urban life Wordsworth uses a great many dynamic verbs, quite frequently participles used adjectivally. Some examples are 'chattering Monkeys'; a 'romping Girl / Bounced, leapt, and paw'd the air'; 'buffoons / Grimacing, writhing, screaming'; and *stumping*; *whirling*; *thumps*; *rattles* and *smites*. Many are in the present tense and a large proportion are aggressive or sordid in connotation. In all these ways, Wordsworth's vocabulary when describing the city opens up a noteworthy new dimension to Wordsworth's diction. Indeed, the fact that he could use this type of vocabulary makes us more appreciative of his usual language, since it is clear that he selected it deliberately from a much wider range than we normally associate with him. One connecting thread, however, is the type of words, which are for the most part basic and everyday. Another is the way in which Wordsworth moves between specific and general vocabulary.

The three long blank verse poems, excluding the cycle of shorter poems on 'The Naming of Places', that appeared in the second edition of *Lyrical Ballads* in 1800, were all composed in their final version in that year. They are less reflective than 'Tintern Abbey' and, therefore, contain a higher proportion of concrete vocabulary. 'The Old Cumberland Beggar', finished in 1800, includes a more diverse array of concrete objects and in consequence more concrete words than the other two. The beggar himself is introduced as seated:

On a low structure of rude masonry.

This is a convoluted way of saying 'a low stone wall' and can be compared with the 'long stone-seat' on which the Priest sits at the beginning of 'The Brothers'. At times Wordsworth denotes concrete objects in rather literary terms in preference to commonly used words and these also convey an impression of the abstract. Further on in the poem, however, the beggar is shown in more straightforward terms in relation to real objects: 'a bag all white with flour'; 'his scraps and fragments' – the defining noun *food* is not mentioned at this point but is sufficiently apparent for it to be clear; 'the crumbs', which 'in little showers / Fell on the ground'. Vocabulary is no barrier to immediate understanding. Other objects of the rural domestic scene are mentioned and almost without exception in concrete, ordinary words: the beggar's hat; the toll-gate; the spinning wheel of the gate-keeper; and the wheels of the mail coach. The landscape is again conveyed through more generalised words, such as *hill*; *dale*; *lane*; *sky*, and another circumlocutory and rather clumsy phrase: 'fields with rural works'. This non-particularised vocabulary of the surrounding countryside, scarcely constituting description, may have a definite purpose: it is not seen by the beggar himself. His vision is restricted to 'one little span of earth': the roadway immediately in front of him, as 'bowbent' (one of Wordsworth's more striking adjectives), he walks along with his eyes on the ground. In contrast to the vagueness of the larger landscape, the details of this narrow area of vision are expressed clearly:

                    some straw,
Some scattered leaf, or marks which, in one track,
The nails of cart or chariot wheel have left
Impressed on the white road in the same line,
At distance still the same.

There is minute attention to detail here but the effect is again diminished by the lack of specifying adjectives, the use of the indefinite pronoun *some* and the openness of the cause of the nail marks, which might have been made by *either* 'cart or chariot'. This is almost certainly a conscious withdrawal of a sense of the specific, maybe because the beggar himself does not notice the objects on which he gazes. None of the words is totally abstract, although the verb *impress* is frequently used by Wordsworth in an abstract or metaphorical sense to denote the working of the mind. Here, however, it is intended in its literal, physical meaning. From this point the words drawn from rural life disappear until the end of the poem. Then, with the exception of the line:

Beat his grey locks against his withered face,

the vocabulary is once more used in a generalised way. The features of the landscape through which the beggar passes, although expressed in ordinary words, are merely representative: *valleys*; *mountain solitudes* (the abstract and literary noun reinforces the generalised sense of place conveyed); and the elements: *wind*; *frosty air*; and *winter snows*. Throughout the descriptive part of the poem, as in 'Tintern Abbey', there is a tension between the particular and the general, both of which are expressed through mainly concrete and certainly everyday vocabulary. The reason for the tension here is rather different although related to that in 'Tintern Abbey': the beggar is one particular beggar for dramatic purposes but he represents all beggars who may be affected by the new legislation for paupers. Even the vivid and dramatically presented picture of the beggar eating is somehow thrown out of focus by the abstract compound *chance-gathered meal* although this again is composed of very basic words. This is an example of compression of vocabulary. In the blank verse poems compression seems to be rarer in the diction than in the syntax.

In most of the blank verse poems Wordsworth occasionally uses a typical eighteenth-century sounding word or idiom. Sometimes there is a possible reason for his reverting to this type of diction, which he used in his early poems in couplets but had by this time deliberately discarded. An example in 'The Old Cumberland Beggar' occurs near the end when we find the periphrastic circumlocution *languid orbs* for 'eyes'. There seems no good reason for this except that it avoids the repetition of *eyes*, which had occurred a few lines before. This is the only instance of this type of diction in this poem. As with the shorter poems in ballad metre, there are occasional words of Old English origin which, because of their obsolescence, sound rather elevated. Instances of these are *dole* (now revived for a specific use in this age of unemployment) and *scrip*, both in relation to the charity shown the beggar by the old women: 'the dole of village dames' and:

> she from her chest of meal
> Takes one unsparing handful for the scrip
> Of this old Mendicant . . .

Mendicant is a rather elevated word, and there are others, although most of the lofty-sounding verse arises again from phrases and words in combination, such as 'a silent monitor' and 'a little grove of their own kindred', where once again the word *grove* gives an eighteenth-century sound to the nominal group. 'His charters and exemptions' is a further instance (one of the phrases from a legal register noted previously) and this is immediately preceded by another example of an Old English word in the phrase 'his peculiar boons'. There is, then, a variety of types of diction in this poem, even though it is mostly the vocabulary of everyday use.

Begun like 'The Old Cumberland Beggar' about two years before, 'The Brothers' was not finished until 1800 when it appeared in the second edition of *Lyrical Ballads*.[11] Here all three groups of words are found.

The setting serves only as the background of the brother's story. The scene is symbolic: a change in the configuration of the landscape, brought about by a thunderbolt, is crucial to the meaning of the poem. This background is, therefore, once more depicted in general rather than specific words. In fact, the poem starts not with a description of the dale at all but with a domestic scene of the Priest and his family. The first mention of the landscape comes nearly a hundred lines further on and is seen in retrospect through Leonard's reaction to it:

> looking round he thought that he perceiv'd
> Strange alteration wrought on every side
> Among the woods and fields, and that the rocks,
> And the eternal hills, themselves were chang'd.

There is nothing of the particular here. The vocabulary is basically concrete but tends once more towards the general. For instance, the brothers' early home is pointed out as 'that single cottage' (the very one but not particularised, like the 'single field' of the 'Intimations Ode') and their family farm as 'those few green fields'. Part of the vocabulary related to the scene is simple and basic: *woods*; *fields*; *rocks* (flowers are mentioned but not specified by name) – but some words, and more than in the previous two poems examined, are elevated and literary in sound, coming from Romance or Latin sources, even though still concrete: *torrent*; *precipice*; *chasm*, and *cataract*. It is, indeed, the language of the Romantic and the picturesque. The word *crag*, which occurs more than once, sounds poetic or literary to many readers nowadays, perhaps, but is in fact of Celtic origin and particularly found in the north of England, where it is still an everyday word. The lack of precise descriptions of particular scenes or parts of the total scene is slightly offset by the more liberal use in this poem of real place names (the location is Ennerdale) especially in the Priest's envisaging of Leonard's possible return:

> From the great Gavel, down by Leeza's Banks,
> And down the Enna, far as Egremont.

Words of the second group, appertaining to rural domestic life, appear in clusters. At the point where the Priest briefly enumerates local happenings of the dale the vocabulary is again general, although concrete:

> then for our own homes!
> A Child is born or christened, a Field ploughed,
> A Daughter sent to service, a Web spun,
> The old House-clock is decked with a new face.

Most of the subjects of the clauses here are introduced by the non-particularising indefinite article, and again there is the non-specific effect of the 'either/or' in 'born or christened'. More specific words and phrases occur at the beginning of the poem when the occupations of the Priest's family are being described. This vocabulary recalls again the detail of description in 'The Ruined Cottage':

> Upon the stone
> His Wife sate near him, teasing matted wool,
> While, from the twin cards toothed with glittering wire
> He fed the spindle of his youngest Child,
> Who turned her large round wheel in the open air
> With back and forward steps,

and again a few lines further on:

> at last,
> Risen from his seat, beside the snow-white ridge
> Of carded wool, which the old man had piled
> He laid his implements with gentle care,
> Each in the other locked.

In description of this kind the nominal groups become longer, with postmodification which includes both prepositional phrases and participial, often present participle, clauses. The words, whether nouns, adjectives or participles, are striking, as well as specific, as in each word of 'twin cards toothed with glittering wire'. The description is made more vivid by the number of clauses, each of which includes a verb, frequently dynamic and lexically fuller than elsewhere, as in '*teasing* matted wool'. More use is made of unusual and precise premodifiers, such as *glittering*. It is not that the individual words are themselves more concrete than usual, but that they are combined into particularised description by the use of more varied parts of speech. This is the point at which vocabulary and syntax meet. From this carefully depicted scene of intimate family life, the Priest goes to meet Leonard, who is locked out of the domestic life of his original home. This may be why Wordsworth is at pains to evoke the picture of quietly busy home life so meticulously.

Another group of words, this time related to life at sea, also appears in this poem, as it does in 'The Female Vagrant' and 'Ruth' (where the vocabulary is altogether more exotic). This is necessary because of the story but not of particular significance in itself and therefore, although concrete, again not particularised. *Piping shrouds*; *the steady sail*; *the broad green wave and sparkling foam*, and other nautical phrases form the setting to Leonard's dreams of:

> the forms of sheep that grazed
> On verdant hills, with dwellings among trees,
> And shepherds clad in the same country grey
> Which he himself had worn.

Again, the vocabulary depicting rural life is concrete but not elaborated or combined to depict a particular scene. The adjective *verdant* used in collocation with the verbs *clad* and *grazed* recalls the eighteenth-century poetic pastoral landscape. Here the use may be deliberate in order to enhance the nostalgia attached to what is essentially a dream belonging to a past era in Leonard's life. 'Forms of sheep' for the single word 'sheep' is another circumlocution. Like all the other nouns in this extract it is in the plural non-individuated form.

The third group of words, those to do with legal affairs and property, are also present in this poem. Again they are essential to the subject matter. Words such as *inheritance*; *interest*; *bond*; *mortgages* and *estate*, all apparently unpoetic words, find a natural place in the context of the narrative.

'Michael' is the last poem in the second edition of *Lyrical Ballads* and was written about the same time as 'The Brothers'.[11] Again it contains all three groups of words, and, like 'The Brothers', the vocabulary used to describe the domestic life of the family combines to produce a vivid and easily visualised individual scene. The rural setting is left undefined, largely through the use of generic words. The description of the dale at the opening of the poem, for instance, is typical rather than individual:

> for beside that boisterous Brook
> The mountains have all opened out themselves,
> And made a hidden valley of their own.
> No habitation there is seen; but such
> As journey thither find themselves alone
> With a few sheep, with rocks and stones, and kites
> That overhead are sailing in the sky.
> It is in truth an utter solitude.

The vocabulary is consistently concrete but mixes ordinary words with those of a more elevated type, such as *habitation* and *solitude*. The many unmodified nouns serve to convey a landscape that could be found anywhere in the Lake District. Only the slightly lengthened nominal group of which the head is *kites* could give a more particular impression if it were used in conjunction with others; on its own it has little individualising effect. This general description can be compared with two vignettes of the family at home. The first comes when the day's work is over and has been quoted earlier (p. 67). Immediately afterwards come the lines:

> when their meal
> Was ended, LUKE........
> And his old Father both betook themselves
> To such convenient work as might employ
> Their hands by the fire-side; perhaps to card
> Wool for the Housewife's spindle, or repair
> Some injury done to sickle, flail, or scythe,
> Or other implement of house or field.

In spite of the tasks being only examples of what the characters *might* do, the number of specific nouns conjures up a clear and intimate scene of domestic activity. The description of the hanging up of the lamp which lights their evening occupations, is, however, symbolic, and like the altered landscape in 'The

Brothers', it mixes elevated, literary words with the more everyday ones:

> Down from the ceiling by the chimney's edge,
> Which in our ancient uncouth country style
> Did with a huge projection overbrow
> Large space beneath, as duly as the light
> Of day grew dim the Housewife hung a Lamp;
> An aged utensil, which had performed
> Service beyond all others of its kind.

The lamp itself, which is described in an appositive nominal group, is denoted by the word *utensil*, which is generic in relation to *lamp*. This enhances its symbolic nature by generalising rather than particularising it. The human connotations of the premodifying adjective *aged* are extended in the following relative clause in which the lamp is made the subject of a human type of action in the verb and complement *performed service*. *Service*, too, is an abstract noun. This type of description is the reverse of the particularising details introduced in other postmodified nominal groups or relative clauses.

An unexpected detail occurs in the description of Luke's growing up:

> the Boy grew up
> A healthy Lad, and carried in his cheek
> Two steady roses that were five years old.

This use of metaphor is again reminiscent of the eighteenth-century diction that Wordsworth had rejected and it seems oddly out of place. The word *rose* used to indicate the health of childhood may be compared with its appearance in the description of the city child, previously quoted (p. 75). The rather exotic effect in 'Michael' is counterbalanced by the unusual premodification, *steady*. The physical soundness of the child contrasts with his later moral instability. This brief description is quite different from the following account of Michael making a crook for the little boy:

> Then Michael from a winter coppice cut
> With his own hand a sapling, which he hooped

With iron, making it throughout in all
Due requisites a perfect Shepherd's Staff.

Here the same method is used as in the description of the
Priest's family in 'The Brothers'. The nominal group, *a sapling*,
is followed by a relative clause which is combined with a
present participial clause to produce a vivid and particularised
object. The nominal groups *winter coppice*; *sapling* and *iron*
collocate with the unusually striking verbs *cut* and *hooped*. The
difference from Wordsworth's usual type of vocabulary is slight
but the effect is marked.

Words to do with legal affairs occur again in 'Michael' and
are, indeed, crucial to this poem as they set in motion the
events leading to the tragic ending. They occur in phrases or in
combination with other words rather than singly. The most
obviously jargon-like legalistic language comes in 'bound in
surety', and 'summoned to discharge the forefeiture'; but there
are related phrases, such as 'a grievous penalty'; 'half his
substance'; and the uncompromisingly unpoetic, 'This unlooked
for claim'.

Attention has been concentrated on these selected groups of
concrete words which seem to be of importance to the meanings
of the poems. The concrete vocabulary is, however, much less
than the abstract. There is a cline from what one might call
truly concrete words, denoting specific objects, towards words
of increasing generalisation and generic words, embracing
wider concepts, until finally complete abstractions are used. An
instance of this was found in the opening lines of 'Tintern
Abbey'. The specificity moved from the word *sycamore* to 'these
orchard-tufts' (the 'unripe fruits' of the trees were mentioned
in the following line) to 'woods and copses', and, finally, all
were subsumed in 'The wild green landscape'. A shorter but
similar example appears in the next verse paragraph, where
the poet moves from rooms to towns and cities. Later, this
becomes even more generalised into *world* in the phrase 'the
fever of the world'. This sequence starts in a less specific way
than the first, since initially no particular room is identified, as
sycamore was a named species of tree. The plural *rooms* signifies
a generalisation, and the word is premodified by an abstract or
transferred adjective *lonely*. The more concrete words tend to

come in clusters and these predictably occur in the more clearly descriptive passages, in direct narration, and also at certain points in conversation. Even here, the proportion of concrete to abstract words varies from poem to poem.

One group of abstract words that has attracted attention is that to do with emotions. These are strictly abstract words, although for Wordsworth emotions were often scarcely more abstract than the objects which evoked them. Josephine Miles says:

> He talked of permanent objects such as lakes and mountains just as he talked of permanent feelings such as love and fear;[12]

and also:

> the names for emotions are in a measure abstract, but it is evident . . . that Wordsworth's treatment of them in context is often concretely figurative and pictorial.[13]

For people of Wordsworth's time emotions were as concrete and as definable as objects accessible to the five senses. Nowadays we expect poetry to rouse emotions either through description or some other means without necessarily stating what the emotion is at all. In the eighteenth and early nineteenth centuries it was enough simply to name the emotion. The details of the object or occasion that had aroused it in the poet were not considered necessary. The act of naming an emotion was sufficient to make the reader feel it as if it had been aroused in a way we should expect today. This is not easy for us now to understand. Our world is made up of particulars, which evoke differing emotional responses; theirs strove after universals, and emotions were thought to be stock responses to given circumstances; they were supposed to be held in common by all men of true feeling and sensibility. That is probably one reason why Wordsworth tended to cut out the details in his revisions of the early poems and moved towards the general in the later poems.

When we come to *The Prelude*, however, in which Wordsworth directly relates his own experiences, much detail is included, and this poem also contains a very high proportion of words denoting emotions. The 'growth of a poet's mind' was as much the growth of his power to feel as of his intellectual development. Amongst the forty-six most used words in *The Prelude* are *love* (used over one thousand times); *hope*; *pleasure*; *joy*; *fear*; *bliss*, and also *happy*. The list also includes the related qualities *peace*; *truth*, and *beauty*.[14] Other words, such as *heart*; *free*, and *power*, especially in collocation with the verb *feel* could be used in a way that indicated a particular emotion. It is worth comparing the words denoting emotions that Wordsworth uses with those listed in Collins's poem, entitled 'The Passions' of 1747. Collins notes directly: *fear*; *anger*; *despair*; *grief*; *hope*; *revenge*; *pity*; *jealousy*; *love*; *hate*; *melancholy*; *cheerfulness*, and *joy*. It is immediately clear that Wordsworth does not name the destructive emotions, such as revenge or jealousy or hate, or even the negative ones, such as melancholy. Fear he does use frequently but in a positive sense of inspiring feelings of awe and even pleasure.

Wordsworth's use of words denoting emotions, however, is not wholly straightforward and frequently differs from that of his predecessors. One thing that applies to all writing is that the vocabulary of emotion may be expressed not only by nouns but also by adjectives and verbs, such as *tranquil* beside *tranquillity* and *grieve* beside *grief*. Of the shorter blank verse poems 'Tintern Abbey' contains the greatest number of words directly stating emotion in various grammatical forms, although this does not mean that emotion is not implied in other ways elsewhere. When, in 'The Brothers', the Priest says of Walter Ewbank that if:

> hauntings from the infirmity of love,
> Are aught of what makes up a mother's heart,
> This old Man in the day of his old age
> Was half a mother to them,

the indirect statement of 'what makes up a mother's heart' indicates an emotion as much as the word *love*. It is therefore far from easy to quantify the amount of vocabulary related to emotion in Wordsworth's poetry although words directly denoting emotions may be readily identified. Similarly we may find intimations of emotion, although again indirectly stated, in the traditional type ballads as well as in the lyrical poems. In 'The Last of the Flock' the line, 'For me it was a woeful day', is as expressive of the emotion the shepherd feels as any denotative noun could be. 'The Thorn' is also concerned with little other than emotions, although it contains few words that directly name one. Again, in 'Michael', to return to the poems in blank verse, the line 'And never lifted up a single stone' is suffused with emotion, although no emotion is named either directly or referred to indirectly. In such ways, therefore, Wordsworth does not always conform to the prevailing notions and practice of his time.

The Prelude, which deals so much with emotion, also shows another facet of Wordsworth's use of emotional vocabulary. He frequently uses the words *passions*; *feelings*; *affections*; *sentiments* and *sensations* but leaves them undefined. In 'Tintern Abbey' he says, 'the sounding cataract / Haunted me like a passion' and leaves it at that. At times he makes it clear that emotions are not capable of definition, as in the passage immediately following the episode of the 'stolen boat' in Book I of *The Prelude*:

> and after I had seen
> That spectacle, for many days, my brain
> Work'd with a dim and undetermin'd sense
> Of unknown modes of being; in my thoughts
> There was a darkness, call it solitude,
> Or blank desertion, no familiar shapes
> Of hourly objects, images of trees,
> Of sea or sky, no colours of green fields;
> But huge and mighty Forms that do not live
> Like living men mov'd slowly through my mind
> By day and were the trouble of my dreams.   (I, 417–27)

Here the natural objects, the trees, sea, sky and fields, are clearly linked in Wordsworth's mind to the turbulent emotions he is experiencing. Another telling passage from Book II is the following:

> I mean to speak
> Of that interminable building rear'd

By observation of affinities
In objects where no brotherhood exists
To common minds.   (II, 401–5)

The first extract shows Wordsworth groping to identify the
thoughts or sensations that he himself felt; in the second he
says that he is trying to convey to others feelings and passions
that are not necessarily felt in common. This is a new departure.
Wordsworth goes beyond the eighteenth-century legacy of
feeling and attempts to broaden it. He was one of the first to
realise that the whole emotional and psychological state of
man's mind is more complex than had hitherto been envisaged
and that the vocabulary for describing the various states of
feeling of which man is capable was deficient.

The importance of emotion in the wider sense was grasped
early by Wordsworth as is seen from a letter he wrote to John
Wilson in June 1802:

> no human being can be ... utterly insensible to the colours,
> forms, or smell of flowers, the [voices?] and motions of birds
> and beasts, the appearances of the sky and heavenly bodies,
> the [genial?] warmth of a fine day, the terror and
> uncomfortableness of a storm, &c. &c. How dead so ever
> many full-grown men may outwardly seem to these thi[ngs],
> all are more or less affected by them, and in childhood, in
> the first practice and exercise of their senses, they must have
> been not the nourish[ers] merely, but often the fathers of
> their passions. There cannot be a doubt that in tracts of
> country where images of danger, melancholy, grandeur, or
> loveliness, softness, and ease prevail, that they will make
> themselves felt, powerfully in forming the characters of the
> people.   (EL, 353–4 [293])

A number of the words denoting emotions are of the type
already seen in the ballads, frequently of Old English stock and
basic, everyday words, such as *love*; *courage*; *strength*; *kindness*,
and *vigour*.[15] Added to these, especially in the contemplative
passages or passages of argument, are many more abstract
words of an elevated or literary type, frequently of Romance
origin, such as *sensation*; *restoration*; *recompense*; *power*; *motion*;

perplexity, and *aspect*. Many of these are formed from verbs and have the endings *-tion* or *-sion*. The adjectives joined to them also often seem abstract, in that they cannot be apprehended by the senses. Examples of these are '*tranquil* restoration'; '*trivial* influence'; '*serene and blessed* mood'; '*sad* perplexity'; '*dreary*' intercourse (of daily life); and '*sober*' pleasure.

Wordsworth uses few verbal adjectives of the active type formed from the present participle in these passages. When he does use a verbally based adjective it is almost always the passive past participle and frequently negative in connotation, as in '*unremembered* pleasure' and 'interest *unborrowed*'. Again Wordsworth frequently mixes native words, often short ones, with borrowed ones. The negative element is represented frequently by the prefix *un-*, as in: '*unintelligible* world' and 'fretful stir *unprofitable*'. A similar affix expressing a kind of negation, or at least a diminishing quality, is the submodifying *half*: '*half-extinguish'd* thought'; *half-create* (attached to a verb); and the syntactically baffling 'That *half-wisdom half-experience* gives' from 'The Old Cumberland Beggar'. *Less* is another negative suffix frequently attached to adjectives: '*houseless* woods'; '*thoughtless* youth'; '*joyless* day-light'. Another way in which Wordsworth negates adjectives is simply by prefixing a negative particle, as in 'nor harsh, nor grating'. This negative manner of expression might easily give the impression that the general effect of Wordsworth's poetry is negative and depressive. This view is reinforced by the fact that Wordsworth frequently chooses the less positive antonym of a pair, as in *sad* instead of *happy*; *dreary* instead of *joyful*. The deduction would, however, be quite wrong, since the poetry is essentially positive and optimistic in its conclusions, even when the positive is based on endurance.

What has been said of nouns and adjectives directly relates to the type of verbs found in the blank verse. These are rarely dynamic and even when active in meaning are more to do with states (even if not strictly stative)[16] than with action itself. This is seen in one of the passages in 'Tintern Abbey' where Wordsworth is recreating direct experience:

> The sounding cataract
> *Haunted* me like a passion.   [My italics]

Even this type of verb is more likely to be rendered by a genuine stative verb, frequently the verb *to be*:

> the tall rock,
> The mountain, and the deep and gloomy wood,
> Their colours and their forms, *were* then to me
> An appetite.   [My italics]

The very casting of this sentence shows Wordsworth's tendency towards nominalisation. The verb *to be* holds a unique place in Wordsworth's vocabulary and often carries a more lexically full and positive sense (or negative as the case may be) than is normal. The best known example is in the line from one of the 'Lucy' poems examined earlier:

> and few could know
> When Lucy ceas'd to be.

'Ceas'd to be', an expanded way of saying *died*, apart from bearing the full meaning of *to be*, is another circumlocutory expression of the type already noted. Occasionally, a more dynamic verb is used, like *bounded* in:

> when like a roe
> I bounded o'er the mountains,

but this is comparatively rare. Typical of the verbs used in 'Tintern Abbey' are *feel*; *see*; *stand*; *mourn*, all unremarkable for they are neither literary nor elevated. Dynamic verbs are often used in a metaphorical sense rather than a literal one, such as *lead* in:

> the affections gently lead us on;

impel in:

> A motion and a spirit, that impels
> All thinking things;

and *hang* in:

> the fretful stir
> Unprofitable, and the fever of the world,
> Have hung upon the beatings of my heart.[17]

Another of these verbs, which has already been mentioned and which occurs frequently in much of Wordsworth's blank verse, is the verb *impress*:

> Once again
> Do I behold these steep and lofty cliffs,
> Which on a wild secluded scene impress
> Thoughts of more deep seclusion.

These lines will scarcely bear a literal interpretation or paraphrase, although the intention is clear. Thoughts are *impressed* on the *mind*, not on the 'wild secluded scene', as the syntax would appear to suggest. As so often with Wordsworth's use of grammatical metaphor, *impress* here is intended in an almost literal sense, although not the physical one as in 'The Old Cumberland Beggar' that was pointed out earlier.

Wordsworth uses relatively few verbs compared with nouns, but he often makes them carry a great deal of weight, although this is not always evident. Many of his verbs, such as those just cited, have metaphorical overtones and others virtually personify natural, or sometimes man-made, objects because they are more usually associated with human agents. Besides these, Wordsworth frequently uses verbs in unusual or unexpected ways. It is no accident that the four verbs commented on above all convey some kind of movement, although only the first, *lead*, is a word that indicates movement in the usual way. *Hang* can be either dynamic or stative but in either sense it is not a verb of movement. Yet in its position in the quotation here it conveys a feeling of movement or, at least, interaction between physical and mental planes of being. This is true of many other verbs which are purely stative. *Feel*, a verb of inert perception, gives a sense of movement and consequently ceases to be entirely stative in 'Tintern Abbey':

> sensations sweet,
> Felt in the blood, and felt along the heart.

Part of the effect is achieved by the unexpected use of the preposition *along*, an unusual syntactic phrasing that is not the only one that Wordsworth uses in this way. Another verb of normally passive connotation, *receive*, acquires a similarly active meaning time after time. Of the Babe in *The Prelude* he writes:

> Thus, day by day,
> Subjected to the discipline of love,
> His organs and recipient faculties
> Are quicken'd, are more vigorous, his mind spreads,
> Tenacious of the forms which it receives.   (II, 250–4)

The nominal form of *receive*, *recipient*, is also included here, and passive and active are constantly intermingled through both verbs and nouns. Later in the same passage *receive* is repeated with the idea of a continuous circularity of movement added:

> From nature largely he receives; nor so
> Is satisfied, but largely gives again.   (II, 267–8)

The passively active becomes directly active. These are all instances of Wordsworth's concept of 'wise passiveness'. Stative verbs, especially those of inert perception, which form a subdivision of stative verbs, are thus pressed into service to convey the interaction and interpenetration between man's mental state and his physical being and surroundings. The reader experiences the workings of the natural world on the movements of the mind and its psychological development through the use of verbs of this type.

The relative scarcity of verbs, therefore, especially in the more contemplative passages of poems such as 'Tintern Abbey' and, above all, *The Prelude*, is balanced by the unobtrusive but pervasive and cumulative semantic weight that Wordsworth pours into them. How these and all other facets of diction in the blank verse poems relate to the sentence structure we shall now examine.

5 Blank Verse – Syntax

The most obvious way in which the sentence structure of Wordsworth's blank verse differs from that of the ballad-type poems and the poems in ballad measure is in sentence length and consequently the complexity of the syntax. The differences are partly the result of the metrical forms. The short stanzas of the ballads prescribed limits to clause and sentence length. Blank verse more readily allows for run-on lines and longer statements. However, even in his blank verse the language of Wordsworth's experimentation in the ballads has left its mark in the shorter sentences interspersed among the longer ones.[1]

Coleridge had made an attempt to write blank verse at least as early as 1794, in a poem addressed to Charles Lamb, and by 1798 he had virtually established his own distinctive style in the form. Apart from his one attempt at drama, *The Borderers* (1796), Wordsworth did not start to write blank verse until 1797, when he began the first parts of what has come to be known as 'The Ruined Cottage' and also 'The Discharged Soldier', which was later worked into *The Prelude*. The early blank verse falls into two sections: that completed early in 1798, just before he began the experimental ballads, and the blank verse poems included in *Lyrical Ballads*. These latter were begun a matter of months or even weeks after the last of the early blank verse pieces and completed at various times.

Syntactical complexity in writing is generally achieved through one of two means: either there are many clauses, usually with a great deal of subordination, which may be sequential or, in a more complex style of writing, placed one within the other like Chinese boxes; or the complexity comes at group level. In this case the nominal groups, usually realising either the subject or, more often, the complement, are expanded extensively. This is chiefly done through postmodification involving both phrases and clauses. The complements of these clauses are in turn frequently postmodified, and prepositional phrases proliferate. One of these two types of writing, with complexities at either the clause or group level almost always accounts for the structure of long sentences and complicated syntax. A writer rarely mixes the two types. With Wordsworth, however, neither of these two modes of writing appears extensively and certainly not with any consistency, although his sentences contain elements of both. With a few exceptions his nominal groups are simple in structure[2] and not unduly lengthened in the ways in which those in Milton's poetry or Jane Austen's prose are. Neither is excessive use of sequential subordinate clauses particularly frequent. There is, however, no doubt that Wordsworth's sentences are often long and his syntax difficult to follow.

One of the most characteristic marks of Wordsworth's blank verse is the separation of the main clause elements, the subject, verb and complement. Often a whole clause, frequently a relative clause, will intervene between subject and verb, as in the following extreme example from 'Michael':

> Fields, where with chearful spirits he had breathed
> The common air; the hills, which he so oft
> Had climbed with vigorous steps; which had impressed
> So many incidents upon his mind
> Of hardship, skill or courage, joy or fear;
> Which like a book preserved the memory
> Of the dumb animals, whom he had saved,
> Had fed or sheltered, linking to such acts,
> So grateful in themselves, the certainty
> Of honorable gains; these fields, these hills
> Which were his living Being, even more
> Than his own blood – what could they less? had laid
> Strong hold on his affections.

Here, there are two subjects – *fields* and *hills* – each expanded in turn. The second subject, *hills*, is followed by three parallel relative clauses. The third has a further typical and quite lengthy expansion of its own. The complement element in this

Here the main clause is preceded by a short subordinate clause. The elements of the main clause itself are not separated: it is the final clause element, the complement, *record* (the direct giving of alms to the beggar, the remembrance of which he embodies), which is expanded. Compression of syntax together with negative means of expression is found in the brief phrase 'Else unremembered', which could easily have been realised in another relative clause ('which would otherwise have been forgotten'). This phrase, in effect, postmodifies the complements of the previous relative clause: 'Past deeds and offices of charity'. The following co-ordinate clause, 'and so keeps alive...', is effectively a relative clause parallel with the first, 'which together binds...', but it is expressed syntactically as a clause dependent upon it, signified by the initial conjunction *so*. It is after this clause that the syntax, and therefore the meaning, become difficult to unravel. The word *hearts*, the complement of the preposition *in* (*in hearts*), which is the postmodifier of *mood* in the *so* clause, is itself postmodified by a relative clause. This is common enough, but here both compression and expansion operate to create confusion. The second co-ordinate subject of this relative clause, which is itself a clause: 'that half-wisdom half-experience gives' is partly realised by a further relative clause in which the relative is again not stated: 'that half-wisdom [which] half-experience gives'. It is *half-experience*, that is experience gained indirectly, presumably in this case by the paying of taxes to help the poor, which gives only *half-wisdom*. The 'lapse of years' and the 'half-wisdom' are followed by the rest of the clause: 'Make slow to feel'. This is again compressed almost to the point of unintelligibility. The *hearts* which will be 'slow to feel' are not restated. The *hearts*, the unstated complement of *make* and the subject of *slow to feel*, a vital link in the double-facing clause, is taken as being understood from two lines back. Furthermore, *hearts* is only *part* of the original postmodified complement, which itself is a postmodifier of the head of the nominal group: 'That kindly mood in hearts'. This makes it even less clear that *hearts* is the full complement of the verb *make*. In fact, if one follows the syntax through logically it should be the 'kindly mood' which is 'slow to feel'. Clearly, Wordsworth means that the 'hearts' are 'slow to feel' 'the kindly mood'. 'The kindly mood' is the complement, again unstated, of the verb *to feel*. The syntax is both so loose and complex that the poet appears almost to have lost control. However, the intention is clear even if the original subject of the clause, *the Villagers*, is so far away that it is virtually out of the reader's mind. The recollection of the human subject makes the metaphor of 'by some sure steps' acceptable, and also the verb *resign*, which is literal, becomes comprehensible. The complement of the verb *resign* is again not stated. What it is precisely, therefore, is uncertain. It is possible that it is once more 'that kindly mood', although the verb may be simply reflexive: they 'resign' themselves. The ambiguity matters little. In spite of the convoluted expression the overall meaning is reasonably clear.

The second way in which Wordsworth lengthens the sentences in his blank verse is by what I have called resumption. Any of the main elements of the clause can be resumed. As with expansion the most frequent element to be resumed is the complement, since the final placing of the complement in normal English word order, S V C, allows for it to be continued more easily without breaking the continuity of the clause. Although Wordsworth uses the complement for resumptive purposes, he also uses the verb, as at the end of the passage from 'Michael', and he also uses the subject. A brief example with resumption of the verb is the following from 'The Brothers', which also, incidentally, illustrates the separation of subject and verb:

> He, thus by feverish passion overcome,
> Even with the organs of his bodily eye,
> Below him, in the bosom of the deep,
> Saw mountains, saw the forms of sheep that grazed
> On verdant hills . . .

The verb *saw* is simply repeated rather than restated with a different word. Another short extract, this time from 'The Old Cumberland Beggar', is an instance of resumption of the subject:

> The easy Man
> Who sits at his own door, and, like the pear

Which overhangs his head from the green wall,
Feeds in the sunshine; the robust and young,
The prosperous and unthinking, they who live
Sheltered, and flourish in a little grove
Of their own kindred, all behold in him
A silent monitor . . .

This is not straightforward resumption, perhaps, so much as a
list of the kinds of people who can profit from the sight of the
beggar going his rounds: 'the easy Man'; 'the robust and
young'; 'the prosperous and unthinking' and 'they who live . . .'.
In 'Tintern Abbey' resumption is frequent. One example
where the complement is the element repeated occurs in:

But oft, in lonely rooms, and 'mid the din
Of towns and cities, I have owed to them, [forms of beauty]
In hours of weariness, sensations sweet,
Felt in the blood, and felt along the heart,
And passing even into my purer mind,
With tranquil restoration: – feelings too
Of unremembered pleasure: such, perhaps,
As may have had no trivial influence
On that best portion of a good man's life,
His little, nameless, unremembered acts
Of kindness and of love.

The 'sensations sweet' become 'feelings', and these are then
repeated in the demonstrative pronoun *such*. The first complement is expanded by participial clauses, two passive and the
third using the present participle *passing*. The first resumption
with the word *feelings*, is very brief: it is simply a postmodifying
prepositional phrase. The second resumption, beginning with
such, is a full clause. The interpersonal *perhaps* and modal
auxiliary *may*, which also expresses the speaker's opinion rather
than an accomplished fact, are indicators of the reflective
quality of the passage. Here, note that the prepositional phrase,
'On that best portion of a good man's life', is again treated in a
resumptive way and expanded in a final lengthy nominal group
placed in apposition. The following sentence which also appears
complex by reason of its length, is constructed on these two

principles of resumption and expansion:

> Nor less, I trust,
> To them I may have owed another gift,
> Of aspect more sublime; that blessed mood,
> In which the burthen of the mystery,
> In which the heavy and the weary weight
> Of all this unintelligible world
> Is lightened.

'That blessed mood' is ostensibly a resumptive complement refining on 'another gift'. This becomes virtually the subject – certainly the grammatical subject – of the relative clauses following it, and when it is again repeated in 'that serene and blessed mood' it is clearly also the theme of the rest of the sentence. In this way Wordsworth is able to forward the argument of his verse through the manipulation of the syntax in a rather unusual way. The lines are as follows:

> that serene and blessed mood,
> In which the affections gently lead us on,
> Until, the breath of this corporeal frame
> And even the motion of our human blood
> Almost suspended, we are laid asleep
> In body, and become a living soul:
> While with an eye made quiet by the power
> Of harmony, and the deep power of joy,
> We see into the life of things.

In this final resumption of the original complement, the relative clause is itself expanded by an adverbial clause beginning with *until*. This, like the basic clause elements S V C, is separated from its two co-ordinate clauses by a lengthy interposed non-finite past participial clause. The actual clauses following *until* are both very short: 'we are laid asleep' and '[we] become a living soul'. This pattern is repeated in the final three lines of the verse paragraph with another adverbial clause, sequential on the *until* clauses. Here, the clause is basically 'While ... we see into the life of things', but again the initiating conjunction *while* is followed, not this time by a non-finite clause, but by a long prepositional phrase, which has been placed initially in the clause and is, therefore, in effect thematically marked. By removing the prepositional adjunct from its more normal final placing, the positive statement, which is the climax of the paragraph, is emphasised. The thematic marking, however, is also significant, since it once more repeats the active passivity through which this vision is achieved and which has been expressed continuously all through these lengthy resumptions and expansions of the original complement, both through the diction and also the mixture of passive and active voices of the verbs.

The two features of expansion and resumption are often found together and have, in the long run, much the same effect. Wordsworth does not rely solely on these two methods for lengthening his sentences. Unlike many writers he uses various different devices, including the more common methods of lengthening nominal groups and constructing elaborate clause complexes, as well as drawing in many prepositional phrases, frequently in juxtaposed groups or strings.

A different way in which Wordsworth lengthens his sentences in the blank verse was mentioned in the previous chapter. This is his use of circumlocutions. Instances of these were 'a low structure of rude masonry'; 'fields with rural works'; and 'her chest of meal' – all from 'The Old Cumberland Beggar'. The first of these quotations (all nominal groups), apart from the additional descriptive adjective *rude*, meaning 'roughly made', was noted as being similar to 'long stone-seat' in 'The Brothers'. The second seems a rather unnecessary circumlocution, since fields are normally indicative of 'rural works'. The prepositional phrase following *fields* could perhaps have been expressed by a premodifying adjective such as *farm* or *cultivated*. We may note here that this phrase appears almost identically in *The Prelude*: 'fields with their rural works', and that it was retained in the 1850 version. This shows how long Wordsworth would hold a phrase in his mind. The published version of 'The Old Cumberland Beggar' was completed in the middle of 1800, although it had existed in an independent state probably since early 1798; Book XII of *The Prelude* was probably not written until after the beginning of 1804 at the earliest. 'Chest of meal' could simply have been inverted to make a compound noun 'meal-chest'. All three examples are expansions which transfer a premodifying adjective or part of a compound noun into a postmodifying prepositional phrase, two of which start with the preposition *of*. Similar instances can be found in the other blank verse poems in *Lyrical Ballads*: from 'The Brothers' – 'the employment of his heart' (thoughts); 'the organs of his bodily eye' (eyes); from 'Michael' – 'hire of praise' (praise); and two more from 'The Old Cumberland Beggar' – 'lapse of years'; and 'necessity of use' (habit). 'Tintern Abbey' actually begins with an example, placed in apposition to its 'short' form:

> Five years have passed; five summers with the length
> Of five long winters!

Other examples occur in 'The Ruined Cottage', written about the same time: 'the after-day of babyhood' and 'the dreary intercourse of daily life'. Many expanded forms occur with the preposition *of* and most could be expressed by a single word, although some of the original meaning might disappear in the contraction. For others a word or words may be omitted altogether, while for some it is not easy to find any exact equivalent. This is shown by the examples just cited from 'The Ruined Cottage'. The language reflects the movements of the mind through speech and into print. What is basically a matter of vocabulary has been expanded into a syntactical construction. This form of expression I shall call 'expanded syntax'.

Some examples of expanded syntactical forms which occur in *The Prelude* are: *the mind of Man*, a phrase which appears fairly frequently instead of the closer-knit and seemingly more forceful 'Man's mind'; *the woods of autumn* for 'autumn woods'; and *were the trouble of my dreams*, where a verb could have been used instead of a noun: 'troubled my dreams'. The alternative expressions for these phrases are numerous. Wordsworth was quite able to express an obvious candidate for the *of* prepositional phrase by another means, as in *autumnal crocus*, which is parallel to 'the woods of autumn', already cited. Another example is *mountain-chapel*, where he uses a compound noun instead of saying 'chapel of the mountain'. One instance where he changes an expanded form to a compound in the 1850 version is *nightfall*, which is substituted for *the fall of night* of the original 1805 text.

The leisurely pace that the expanded syntax gives to the lines, together with other devices that Wordsworth uses, such as a large number of adverbial phrases and clauses of time and place, inculcate the rhythm of 'once upon a time'. This pattern can be seen in the opening of 'Michael':

> Upon the forest-side in Grasmere Vale
> There dwelt a Shepherd, Michael was his name;
> An old man, stout of heart, and strong of limb,
> His bodily frame had been from youth to age
> Of an unusual strength.

This is not the beginning of the poem itself but the part which leads to the story which the narrator/poet is about to relate. Here, there are three examples of expanded syntax involving *of* in four and a half lines, an extremely dense use of them. The leisurely tempo is consequently very obvious. The first two expanded forms, *stout of heart* and *strong of limb*, could be replaced by compounds, 'stout-hearted' and 'strong-limbed'. These are adjectival rather than nominal groups. *His bodily frame* could have been expressed by the single word 'body' or 'physique', and the last line could have been reduced to 'unusually strong', replacing the nominal group with an adjectival one. Indeed, the whole of the last clause is virtually a repetition of *strong of limb*. The slowing down of the lines in this way does not merely set the pace for the events which are to follow: it helps to create the mood of reflection which is an intrinsic part of the tale, even though it purports to be narrative.

One way in which the expanded *of* forms help to produce this mood of reflection and recollection is by separating the quality of an object from the object itself.[3] In sequence of time there is the object, a space filled by *of*, and then the quality appertaining to the object. Such is *woods of autumn* from *The Prelude*. Alternatively, as in the first two examples from 'Michael' the position is reversed: the quality is stated before the object to which it belongs, as in *stout of heart*. This step by step unfolding of the meaning is perhaps more obvious when the verse is spoken than when it is read silently, but it is certain that Wordsworth would have been very conscious of the auditory effect. The spacing achieved by this type of syntax forces the reader to dwell on the detail, which is thereby given added prominence. In the brief extract from 'Michael', we are encouraged to pause and assimilate the circumstances surrounding the story as Wordsworth tells us he himself pondered over them when he first heard it as a boy. In the introductory lines, which come immediately before those quoted, he says:

> the gentle agency
> Of natural objects led me on to feel
> For passions that were not my own, and think
> (At random and imperfectly indeed)
> On man, the heart of man, and human life.

It is no accident that another example of expanded syntax occurs in the last line here: *the heart of man.* Wordsworth's absorption in the tale at the time was probably unconscious, or at most half-conscious; it is only in retrospect that he can bring its action on his mind fully to the surface. The mood of reflection which the poet forces on us is of this submerged kind, for we are largely unconscious of the way the syntax affects our response to the poetry.[4]

The use of participial clauses, especially the passive past participle type, in the expansion of subject and complement, has been mentioned in the course of discussing various examples. There is a strong element of passivity in the syntax of Wordsworth's blank verse, which complements the pervading mood of much of his poetry: 'the wise passiveness', referred to in 'Expostulation and Reply'. The verbs are frequently in the passive voice and these forms occur most, as one might expect, in the reflective verse.

There are other syntactical devices, as well as the choice of vocabulary and verb forms, which contribute to this sense of passiveness. One is the use of inanimate or non-human objects as the subject of a clause. This again is a feature taken up from the earlier blank verse and it occurs also in the early poems in couplets. *An Evening Walk* (1787–9) is particularly full of subjects of this kind but they are deployed differently from the way Wordsworth uses them in the blank verse. In this early poem, most, although combined with metaphor, are merely descriptive and have no effect on man, except occasionally on his physical actions, as in:

> But now the sun had gain'd his western road,
> And eve's mild hour invites my steps abroad.   (87–8)

One can see a shift beginning in *Descriptive Sketches* (1791–2), first published in 1793 and also in couplets. Here there is just a hint of the power that natural objects can have on the mind. It is, however, only a hint and so slight that it may easily be missed among the profusion of personifications and typically eighteenth-century diction. Wordsworth himself drew out this change in the later version published in 1842. The clearest example in the first version comes near the end of the poem:

> Each clacking mill, that broke the murmuring streams,
> Rock'd the charm'd thought in more delightful dreams,
> Chasing those long long dreams the falling leaf
> Awoke a fainter pang of moral grief.   (766–9)

The works of nature begin to affect man's inner self. In the course of revising the poem for publication in 1842 Wordsworth rewrote many passages and these show clearly the way in which his mind and imagination had grown since 1793. For instance, there is a seemingly slight but significant adjustment in some lines about the quiet of Sunday among the mountains. In the first version the stillness is:

> Broke only by the melancholy sound
> Of drowsy bells for ever tinkling round;
> Faint wail of eagle melting into blue
> Beneath the cliffs, and pine-woods steady sugh;
> The solitary heifer's deepen'd low;
> Or rumbling heard remote of falling snow.   (434–9)

In the later version the sound of bells has been changed from *Broke* to *accords*, and they are *soothing* rather than *melancholy*. Most telling of all, two lines have been inserted at the end:

> All motions, sounds and voices, far and nigh,
> Blend in a music of tranquillity.   (362–3)

The various slight changes have all been leading up to the

notion of universal harmony expressed in this final couplet,
which does not appear at all in the version of 1793.

The use of inanimate subjects occurs extensively in 'The
Ruined Cottage', although many of them are still of the descriptive metaphorical type found in *An Evening Walk*. Some short
examples are the following:

> the sun was mounted high.
> Along the south the uplands feebly glared
> Through a pale steam and all the northern downs
> In clearer air ascending shewed their brown
> And [   ] surfaces distinct with shades
> Of deep embattled clouds that lay in spots
> Determined and unmoved;

> some huge oak whose aged branches make
> A twilight of their own;

> a ruined Cottage, four clay walls
> That stared upon each other.

A similar example comes at the beginning of 'The Discharged
Soldier', where it is the windings of the road which reveal the
soldier to the poet:

> It chanc'd a sudden turning of the road
> Presented to my view an uncouth shape
> So near, that, slipping back into the shade
> Of a thick hawthorn, I could mark him well,
> Myself unseen.

There are numerous instances in the poems in *Lyrical Ballads*
which we have already looked at. A typical example is found in
'Michael', where the lamp, from which the shepherd's cottage
takes its name, 'The Evening Star', is repeatedly the subject of
successive clauses:

> as duly as the light
> Of day grew dim, the House-wife hung a lamp;
> An aged utensil, which had perform'd
> Service beyond all others of its kind.

Early at evening did it burn and late,
Surviving Comrade of uncounted Hours
Which going by from year to year had found
And left the Couple neither gay perhaps
Nor chearful . . .

In the line 'Early at evening did it burn and late' the use is normal and expected, but it is in the other clauses that it is noteworthy. In these the lamp is treated as if it is capable of the actions normally performed only by human beings; it is virtually personified. It is not quite clear whether the lamp or the 'uncounted Hours' is the subject of the final clause, but either way the subject, to which is ascribed human-type actions, though inanimate, is the actor through which the life of the couple is revealed, as if it were an observer of the world's comings and goings. The relative clause 'which had perform'd / Service . . .' recalls Coleridge's frost, which 'performs its secret ministry' in 'Frost at Midnight'. This type of personification, which is a kind of metaphor, is far removed from the eighteenth-century personification of abstractions that both Wordsworth and Coleridge had left behind. With Wordsworth it is very frequent and more often occurs in conjunction with nature or natural phenomena than with domestic objects. In the passage quoted earlier, describing Michael's upland home (p. 94) it is also present. It is mainly through the accumulation of verbs of the type used here of the lamp – verbs that are usually associated with human agents – that Wordsworth builds the personification and personalisation of nature into the very fabric of his verse. This type of unemphatic rhetoric which could so easily be missed is found everywhere throughout the blank verse.

In 'Tintern Abbey' natural objects and the forces of nature work on the mind as if they had human powers. Wordsworth thus develops an aspect of the view first seen in *Descriptive Sketches*. One of the best known passages affords the clearest example:

I have felt
A presence that disturbs me with the joy
Of elevated thoughts; a sense sublime

Of something far more deeply interfused,
Whose dwelling is the light of setting suns,
And the round ocean and the living air,
And the blue sky, and in the mind of man
A motion and a spirit, that impels
All thinking things, all objects of all thought,
And rolls through all things.

The complement of the first clause, 'A presence', is the non-human agent which, becoming the actor of the following restrictive relative clause, affects the poet's mind. It is resumed after the semi-colon in 'a sense sublime' and is again subjected to resumption in 'A motion and a spirit' five lines further on. The 'sense sublime', although not itself the subject of any verb, is first given the normally human attribute of having a 'dwelling'[5] and then, in the resumption, becomes both a 'motion', an abstract noun which, for Wordsworth, attracts a dynamic verb,[6] and also a 'spirit', which is one part of the human condition. It is therefore capable of 'human' activities of a selected kind. The abstract and inanimate 'presence' has thus been transformed into something that shares, or even transcends, active human powers.

Another way in which Wordsworth both creates a sense of passivity in the human beings in his poems and also stresses the peculiarly active force of normally inanimate objects is through his use of transitive and intransitive verbs. This is true both in his blank verse and in the various types of ballads. Intransitive verbs such as *go*; *sit*, and *cry* from 'The Thorn' (all repeated more than once), as well as *creep* and *strive* are frequent. In 'Tintern Abbey' we find *stand*; *come*, and *bound*. Transitive verbs are often used intransitively. Examples in 'The Thorn' are *blow*; *cut*, and *sweep*; and in 'Tintern Abbey' *turn*; *hang*; *roll* and *lead*. In addition, the high proportion of copula verbs, including the verb *to be* has already been noted. This results in a lack of movement and a withdrawal of the normal active force which both animate and inanimate objects exert over each other in the external world. The poetry appears static and inert. But when dynamic verbs are used transitively they frequently operate on internal feelings. This is particularly true of 'Tintern Abbey' where verbs such as *disturb* and *impel* are used in this way. This last use nearly always occurs with an inanimate subject and is closely linked to the passive, where an inanimate agent is usually implied, as in 'an eye made quiet'. All these verbal uses reflect Wordsworth's preoccupation with states of mind rather than with physical activity.[7]

Another factor contributing to the sense of passivity in Wordsworth's poems is one that has frequently been mentioned already and that is the various means of negative expression which he uses. Whole statements are expressed negatively when a positive meaning is intended; negative conjunctions, such as *nor*, are frequently used; and individual words are negated or diminished by prefixes. Wordsworth rarely says 'often' when he can say 'not seldom'. Such negative expressions can be illustrated from the opening of 'Michael'. After setting the scene of the poem in positive terms, Wordsworth introduces the tale negatively:

> Nor should I have made mention of this Dell
> But for one object which you might pass by,
> Might see and notice not.

The initial negative statement of this quotation is followed by a positive sentence, relating to the 'object' which the passer-by might 'notice not', and this, in turn, is followed by another stating that a story attaches to the stones. The nature of the story is further indicated by two subsequent statements; the first is expressed positively but, through the negative prefix *un-* of 'unfinished' (there are three *un-* prefixes in four lines), becomes negative – the tale, apparently, is not concerned with 'events'; the second is semantically positive but expressed through two negatives, the prefix *un-* again and the negation of that adjective, 'not unfit':

> beside the brook
> There is a straggling heap of unhewn stones!
> And to that place a story appertains,
> Which, though it be ungarnished with events,
> Is not unfit, I deem, for the fire-side,
> Or for the summer shade.

Michael, himself, who 'had not passed his days in singleness', another negatively expressed statement of positive meaning, is almost wholly described in positive terms, but Wordsworth does not need to use grammatical negatives to express a statement negatively:

> And grossly that man errs who should suppose
> That the green Valleys and the Streams and Rocks
> Were things indifferent to the Shepherd's thoughts.

Here, the first statement is negative in meaning, although expressed positively, but the ultimate meaning is positive because of the negative word *indifferent*. Basically, the statement means: 'It would be right to assume that "the green Valleys", "Streams" and "Rocks" were things of great significance in the shepherd's inner life', as well as in his physical life and livelihood. Wordsworth achieves a positive meaning through using two semantically negative words – a verbal double negative. Naturally, as indicated, many of the statements are positive – a passage of any length would be impossible without them – but there is considerably more negative expression in Wordsworth's poetry than in that of most other writers and it is a hall-mark of his language.

Since repetition is a feature of Wordsworth's ballad poems that he found necessary to comment on in his 1800 Note to 'The Thorn', it is not surprising that he used it also in the blank verse. A typical passage in which it occurs is the following from 'The Old Cumberland Beggar':

> He travels on, a solitary Man,
> His age has no companion. *On the ground*
> His eyes are turned, and as he *moves along*
> They *move along the ground*; and, evermore,
> Instead of common and habitual sight
> Of fields with rural works, of hill and dale,
> And the blue sky, one little span of earth
> Is all his prospect. Thus from day to day,
> Bowbent, his eyes for ever *on the ground*,
> He plies his weary journey.   [My italics]

The various words, phrases and parts of clauses which are repeated have been printed in italics for ease of recognition. Some, such as *on the ground*, are repeated more than once. The first line is itself an exact repetition of a line occurring earlier in the verse paragraph. Other phrases or clauses are not repeated exactly but the meaning is repeated in different words, such as 'He plies his weary journey', which echoes 'He travels on'. The insistence on the same, or similar, words and phraseology has various effects. In 'The Old Cumberland Beggar' it seems to emphasise and draw attention to the monotony of the beggar's life and his restricted view of the world.

In the blank verse poems of early 1798, as well as the rhyming poems of the same period, such as 'The Female Vagrant', extracted from 'Salisbury Plain',[8] the syntax and style are relatively undifferentiated, both between separate poems and in the course of one poem. 'The Ruined Cottage', the story of Margaret, which was later to become the second half of Book I of *The Excursion*, is ostensibly narrative. It is not, however, straight narrative and becomes a series of descriptions of changing states of mind, the changing psychological moods of Margaret each time the Pedlar visits her home after the disappearance of her husband. There is, therefore, little action – one should notice Wordsworth's introductory line, a line that foreshadows the opening to the tale of Michael:

> 'Tis a common tale
> By moving accidents uncharactered.

'The Ruined Cottage' went through many drafts and the language changed considerably during the course of composition. The concrete diction and particularised descriptions of the original version have already been noted. Syntactically, a large number of the sentences are short and not very complex. Where sentences are lengthened, the lengthening is done in the manner described earlier: through resumption and expansion. The general trend is towards assertive statement and even in its more speculative passages the syntax lacks the reasoning found in the later reflective type verse, such as 'Tintern Abbey'. Interpersonal elements are not in evidence, which partly accounts for the sense of a lack of argument, and there are few subordinate clauses with the introductory conjunctions usual in reasoned discourse, such as *and so* or *therefore*. In 'The Ruined Cottage' long sentences occur mainly in a part hitherto little mentioned: the early account of the Pedlar.[9] Here some subordination does occur. This is fitting since it is not mere description but one of the earliest accounts of the effect of Nature on the mind of man. It is the beginning of what has become known as Wordsworth's 'philosophy' and is more fully expressed, in relation to the poet himself, in 'Tintern Abbey'. Later it was to figure extensively in *The Prelude*. A certain amount of subordination also occurs in 'The Discharged Soldier'. Both poems have a great deal of co-ordination – more than most of the later blank verse poems. 'The Ruined Cottage' is both assertive and positive, with relatively little negation or expression conveying the various types of passivity that Wordsworth uses in his later blank verse. Negatives and passives do occur but not in the typical Wordsworthian way of expressing something active and positive through negative or passive means. The negatives are mostly in the tragic part of Margaret's tale, and this parallels to some extent, although on a more literal and less symbolic plane, the ending of the tale of Michael. There are more negatives of the type we usually associate with Wordsworth, and also passive expression of the types already discussed, in the description of the Pedlar:

> To him was given an ear which deeply felt
> The voice of Nature ...

There is just a hint of the repetition which Wordsworth later developed extensively. Repetition is used more often in 'The Discharged Soldier', but it is somewhat different from that found in the later poems. It is scattered and not always literal repetition. Near synonyms or synonymous expressions and similar structures are used. These wake echoes in the reader's mind, which are different from the emphasis achieved through the later forms of direct repetition. Thematic marking occurs extensively in both these early poems. Rarely does a sentence or clause begin with its subject. Very often a prepositional phrase comes first and sometimes a subordinate clause. Unmarked themes usually occur at those parts of the poems

that are straightforward narrative or directly descriptive.
Wordsworth's increasing use of inanimate subjects in the early
poems to affect human sensibility has already been
demonstrated and need not be discussed further. One feature,
only briefly mentioned before, is the use of compressed or
elliptical syntax. This is characteristic of Wordsworth's composition as a whole. It is occasionally found in both 'The Ruined
Cottage' and 'The Discharged Soldier' and usually takes the
form of a phrase or non-finite clause, often a past participle
clause, reminiscent of the Latinate or Miltonic constructions
found more often in Wordsworth's early verse.[10] An example
from 'The Discharged Soldier' is:

> At this he stoop'd,
> And from the ground took up an oaken Staff;
> By me yet unobserv'd.

Here, the phrase 'By me yet unobserv'd' would more naturally
be expressed in English by a relative clause: 'which was
unobserved by me'. A similar kind of ellipsis occurs in 'The
Ruined Cottage':

> A while on trivial things we held discourse,
> To me soon tasteless.

The same kind of compression is found in 'Tintern Abbey'.
One example is:

> other gifts
> Have followed, for such loss, I would believe,
> Abundant recompence.

Here, the compressed phrase 'for such loss ... Abundant
recompence' has again no verb. This could also be filled out by
a relative clause: 'which have been ...'.
'Tintern Abbey' contains all the syntactic features characteristic of Wordsworth's blank verse. In this poem Wordsworth
brings together all the structures and devices that he had
previously used sporadically. There is, however, some variation
within the poem itself. Negation, for instance, in the sense

discussed in this chapter, begins only after the first verse paragraph, which sets the scene in positive terms. The negatives start at the point where Wordsworth begins to disclose the true import that the remembrance of the scene in front of him has had over the years, the influence of Nature on his mind and development. They continue virtually through the rest of the poem, although it finishes with an affirmation:

> these steep woods and lofty cliffs,
> And this green pastoral landscape, were to me
> More dear, both for themselves, and for thy sake.

Here we have the exact repetition of the nominal group 'steep and lofty cliffs' that appeared at the beginning of the poem. The structure of the poem has come full circle and its careful shaping can easily be overlooked. Another, earlier, statement:

> Therefore am I still
> A lover of the meadows and the woods,

shows Wordsworth's tendency towards nominalisation. It could have been phrased 'I still love' but Wordsworth chooses instead a structure that changes the verb into an abstract noun. In 'Tintern Abbey' Wordsworth also uses many interpersonal phrases and clauses, such as 'I trust'. This is chiefly because the sentiments expressed are those of the speaker himself. However, this structure adds to the effect of a reasoned and reflective type of verse which is the dominant mood of the poem. There is, too, much more subordination than in the earlier poems, and more clauses introduced by conjunctions such as *so*; *therefore*; *though*, and *for* in the sense of 'because'. The sentences are generally long and there is much resumption, examples of which have been quoted, and by means of which Wordsworth forwards his argument. Verbs are amazingly few – the clauses are often lengthened to a surprising extent – and many of the verbs which do occur are stative or at least non-dynamic. At the point where Wordsworth attempts to recreate the experience of five years before when he first visited this part of the River Wye, the style changes perceptibly for a short time:

> when like a roe
> I bounded o'er the mountains, by the sides
> Of the deep rivers, and the lonely streams,
> Wherever nature led; more like a man
> Flying from something that he dreads than one
> Who sought the thing he loved. For nature then
> To me was all in all. – I cannot paint
> What then I was. The sounding cataract
> Haunted me like a passion.

Initially the verbs are dynamic and the sentences more truly positive. Incidentally, one might note the re-appearance of the first clause some two years later in 'The Brothers':

> Like roe-bucks they went bounding o'er the hills.

This extraordinary repetition, not only of the biblical image, but almost exactly in the same words, shows again how Wordsworth retained in his mind words and phrases over long periods of time. Although different in the ways mentioned from other parts of 'Tintern Abbey' the majority of the clauses in this passage are still fairly long and resumption is still used. In spite of the more active participation of the poet, characterised by the first person personal pronouns in subject case, there are two natural actors, 'nature' itself and then 'the sounding cataract'. Immediately after these lines the syntax shifts back into the passive/negative mode:

> the tall rock,
> The mountain, and the deep and gloomy wood,
> Their colours and their forms, were then to me
> An appetite: a feeling and a love,
> That had no need of a remoter charm.

Thus, in 'Tintern Abbey' we see Wordsworth developing the syntactic means of expression that were already present in the early 1798 blank verse and turning it to the purpose for which he was later to use it more fully in *The Prelude*.

The three full-length poems in blank verse that appeared in the 1800 edition of *Lyrical Ballads* contain most of the typically

Wordsworthian syntactical features. 'The Old Cumberland Beggar'[11] has relatively little subordination compared even with the
other blank verse. Because Wordsworth was introducing an
argument against the introduction of the proposed reforms to
the Poor Laws the sentences tend to be more directly assertive.
It is one of the most sociological poems in *Lyrical Ballads* and its
power is notably heightened by compressed syntax. Thematic
marking of a particular kind is used in this poem. It takes the
form of placing the complement, especially if it is a personal
pronoun, in theme position. It is not surprising that
Wordsworth resorts to this device several times here, for it
helps him to keep the beggar as the theme or subject of
discourse. So, we find the Latinate construction:

Him from my childhood have I known

and:

Him even the slow-pac'd waggon leaves behind.

'The Brothers' and 'Michael' show an interesting contrast in
the distribution of syntactic features. Both contain the usual
features already discussed and both are basically narrative in
the main body of the poem. But the presentation is markedly
different. 'The Brothers' is mostly in dramatic form with dialogue, whereas 'Michael' is related in traditional manner by an
external narrator. 'Michael', however, also contains a fair proportion of dialogue, presented by means of the usual narrative
conventions. It is in these parts that the two poems differ most
in their syntax and also in their vocabulary. The dialogue in
'The Brothers' is, on the whole, elevated in tone with rather
literary and stilted-sounding diction for everyday discourse
and the sentence structure of the speeches is correspondingly
complex, as in:

You recollect I mention'd
A habit which disquietude and grief
Had brought upon him, and we all conjectur'd
That, as the day was warm, he had lain down
Upon the grass, and waiting for his comrades

> He there had fallen asleep, that in his sleep
> He to the margin of the precipice
> Had walked, and from the summit had fallen head-long.

Although part of the vocabulary is commonplace, such words as *disquietude*; *conjectur'd*; *margin*, and *precipice* are not usually found in everyday conversation. Similarly, the interpolation of the prepositional phrase 'to the margin of the precipice' between the subject and verb sounds unnatural. The actual deviations from ordinary usage here are comparatively slight quantitatively but they heighten the whole. Another passage which one might expect to display the same elevated expression is the description of the splitting of the cliff in a thunderstorm but instead the wording here is much more commonplace:

> On that tall pike,
> (It is the loneliest place of all these hills)
> There were two Springs which bubbled side by side,
> As if they had been made that they might be
> Companions for each other: ten years back,
> Close to those brother fountains, the huge crag
> Was rent with lightning – one is dead and gone,
> The other, left behind, is flowing still.

It must be remembered that, apart from the near Gothick nature of the event described, the whole passage is symbolic and, therefore, outside the ordinary run of discourse although spoken by the Priest. Yet both the vocabulary and syntax of these lines are relatively simple and straightforward. The word *bubbled*, in particular – a very ordinary if expressive word – seems to conjure up the high spirits of the two boys whom the 'brother fountains' represent. The sentence structure is some of the most straightforward in Wordsworth's verse and scarcely deviates from the normal S V C A order. Even the interpolated sentence in parenthesis seems a natural feature of spontaneous conversation. In contrast a short description of Walter Ewbank's love for his two grandsons sounds unnatural:

> and if tears
> Shed, when he talk'd of them where they were not,

And hauntings from the infirmity of love,
Are aught of what makes up a mother's heart,
This old Man in the day of his old age
Was half a mother to them.

The elliptical 'where they were not', the rather semantically opaque 'infirmity of love', collocating with the unexpected word *hauntings*, the prepositional complement clause 'of what makes up a mother's heart' and finally the circumlocution of 'the day of his old age' show idiom and syntax combining to produce a highly wrought speech that one would be unlikely to hear in everyday life. Wordsworth had already had practice in writing dialogue in *The Borderers*, his blank verse play written mainly in 1796 and finished early in 1797. That experience was not without results. There are dramatic touches in the dialogue of 'The Brothers' that allow the reader to visualise the reactions of the two men, particularly those of Leonard. The Priest does most of the talking and many of Leonard's interruptions are cut short. These exchanges impart a sense of genuine dialogue to the poem. For instance, the different preoccupations of the two men are evident in the following passage, where the Priest ignores the eager prompting of Leonard for news of his younger brother:

PRIEST
But Leonard –
LEONARD
Then James still is left among you –
PRIEST
'Tis of the elder Brother I am speaking.

The Priest's words indicate Leonard's reactions again in the following lines, which are also dramatically ironic:

If you weep, Sir,
To hear a stranger talking about strangers,
Heaven bless you when you are among your kindred!

There is, therefore, a curious mixture of the highly stylised and the realistically dramatic in the dialogue. In 'Michael' there

is altogether more consistent differentiation in the syntax of
the various parts. Some of the narrative has already been
examined. In the conversation, especially that between Michael
and his son, Luke, the sentences, if not always short, are usually
straightforward in structure and the vocabulary distinctly non-
literary, as in these lines:

> in the open fields my life was pass'd
> And in the mountains, else I think that thou
> Hadst been brought up upon thy father's knees.
> – But we were playmates, Luke; among these hills,
> As well thou know'st, in us the old and young
> Have play'd together . . .

They have the straightforwardness of speech. Another short
extract shows the same characteristic:

> 'Till I was forty years of age not more
> Than half of my inheritance was mine.
> I toil'd and toil'd; God bless'd me in my work,
> And 'till these three weeks past the land was free.

The speeches themselves are often long and there is at times
the same circumlocution that marks the extracts quoted from
'The Brothers', as in:

> though now old
> Beyond the common life of man, I still
> Remember them who lov'd me in my youth.
> Both of them sleep together: here they liv'd
> As all their Forefathers had done, and when
> At length their time was come, they were not loth
> To give their bodies to the family mold.

Wordsworth's negative, and circumlocutory, form of expression
appears in the last clause. The circumlocutions lift the speech
and lend a dignity to the old man which makes the final
tragedy much more poignant. The conversation is not wholly
realistic but the vocabulary and sentence structure are basically
more straightforward than those of the speeches in 'The

Brothers'. At the climax of this lengthy parting, when the sheepfold is introduced, Michael's sentences are short and extremely simple:

> This was a work for us and now, my Son,
> It is a work for me. But lay one Stone –
> Here, lay it for me, Luke, with thine own hands.
> I for the purpose brought thee to this place.

In 'Michael' simplicity of language raises the emotional level. Different syntactical features interweave throughout the poem. At the beginning where Wordsworth is both describing the setting and explaining the effect the tale had on him as a boy, the full range of features that he uses most are present. Some of these disappear, however, once the tale itself begins. The expanded syntactical forms which we examined earlier in the chapter begin to disappear when the narrative proper starts nearly half-way through the poem at line 217:[12]

> While this good household thus were living on
> From day to day, to Michael's ear there came
> Distressful tidings.

This matter-of-fact quality in the syntax reaches its height in the account of Luke's fall:

> Meantime Luke began
> To slacken in his duty, and at length
> He in the dissolute city gave himself
> To evil courses: ignominy and shame
> Fell on him, so that he was driven at last
> To seek a hiding-place beyond the seas.

The brevity of this catastrophic development in the tale can be accounted for by the fact that it is only the cause of the real tragedy. The language used gives the appearance of treating it almost dismissively. One reason for the prosaic sound of the verse here is the carefully varied incidence of the caesura in each line and the irregular stress patterns. From this point in the poem Michael is viewed from without. The narrator steps back into the tale and the use of the first person pronoun, together with interpersonal comments, such as "'tis believed by all', have the effect of distancing the reader from the shepherd. Diction and syntax become increasingly factual and straightforward towards the end of the poem. The final sentences are comparable with those of 'The Brothers' in their flatness. There is a similarity, too, in what may be called the climactic statements of the two poems. Both come a short way before the end. The climax of 'The Brothers' is not easy to place and it may be that the poem has no single climax. The final comment on the younger lad's death is made by Leonard, when in the fullness of his emotion he utters the brief words 'My Brother'. This moment of intensity is immediately lowered by the narrator's matter-of-fact comment, 'The Vicar did not hear the words'. This climax of the brothers' tragedy may easily pass unnoticed. The poem rushes on to the present preoccupations of the Priest. To see the effect in context it is necessary to quote the passage in full:

> The Priest here ended –
> The Stranger would have thank'd him, but he felt
> Tears rushing in; both left the spot in silence,
> And Leonard, when they reach'd the church-yard gate,
> As the Priest lifted up the latch, turn'd round,
> And, looking at the grave, he said, 'My Brother.'
> The Vicar did not hear the words: and now,
> Pointing towards the Cottage, he entreated
> That Leonard would partake his homely fare:
> The other thank'd him with a fervent voice,
> But added, that, the evening being calm,
> He would pursue his journey. So they parted.

The muted tone of this parting, which is also Leonard's parting from the dreams and hopes that have sustained him in his wanderings, is comparable with the equivalent climax of 'Michael'. There also, incidentally, the ultimate tragedy, although not likely to pass unnoticed this time, is expressed through a negative:

and 'tis believed by all
That many and many a day he thither went,
And never lifted up a single stone.

This statement, with the overwhelming simplicity of its final
clause, is one of the greatest achievements of Wordsworth's
blank verse and the point towards which his linguistic experimentation had been working. The last few lines that follow
merely round off details, as at the end of 'The Brothers'. By
the very contrast of the final prosaic comments emotion is
lowered and, at the same time, the bare simplicity of the
language used at the preceding moment of tragedy is heightened. There is no philosophising or comment. The stark return
to everyday reality speaks for itself in concrete diction and
simple prose-like sentences. The moments of climax in the two
poems are not unlike the equivalent lines, examined in Chapter
3, from the 'Matthew' poems. There, too, the climax on each
occasion, when Matthew rejected any renewal of the past or
chance to recover what he had lost, was expressed in simple
diction in normal prose order and by means of a negative.
Wordsworth seems to reserve the most simple, straightforward
linguistic expression for the highest points of his poetry.

6 Coleridge

Coleridge's reputation rests on comparatively few poems and it would be hard to find a poet who has left more pieces unfinished. It is impossible to say whether he would now be remembered as a poet at all had he not met Wordsworth. He had other literary friends, among them Charles Lamb and Robert Southey, who became his brother-in-law, but it was after his meeting with Wordsworth in 1795 and his close association with the poet and his sister, which began in 1797, that his poetic talent had its brief flowering. The poems for which he is remembered fall into three groups: the purely magical, represented by *Kubla Khan*; the short blank verse poems, known as the 'conversation' poems and mostly written about 1798; and the ballad or medieval-type poems, such as *Christabel* and *The Ancyent Marinere*.

Coleridge was as deeply interested in language as Wordsworth, as his prose writings show. At times he had an even greater facility in the use of words and sounds, although he lacked the persistence that resulted in Wordsworth's much larger output of great poetry. Coleridge's linguistic inventiveness was certainly more striking than Wordsworth's. At the age of twenty-one he ran away from Cambridge, probably to escape his creditors, and joined the dragoons. Still keeping his own initials, he enlisted under the name of Silas Tomkyn Comberbache. However, army life did not suit him and he appealed to his brothers to buy him out. What made him choose such a preposterous name? We learn from his letters that he disliked his own first name. In 1804 he wrote to Southey:

such a vile short plumpness, such a dull abortive smartness, in [the] first Syllable, & this so harshly contrasted by the obscurity & indefiniteness of the syllabic Vowel, & the feebleness of the uncovered liquid, with which it ends . . . altogether it is perhaps the worst combination, of which vowels and consonants are susceptible. (*Letters*, II, 1126)

It is not easy to see how the first syllables of *Tomkyn* and *Comberbache* were much improvement on *Sam*. Coleridge, however, was clearly very sensitive to sounds and their associations. This branch of language study has never received much attention and, indeed, most linguists today would agree that sounds contain no intrinsic meaning, any associations which they may arouse being purely subjective. One of the most recent proponents of that branch of linguistic theory known as phonostylistics was the Russian born Roman Jakobson (1896–1982), a leading structuralist.[1] Any given language can contain words that have a particular combination of sounds which have certain connotations in common. In English, for example, many words beginning with the sounds 'fl' denote movement: *flicker*; *flutter*; *flare*; *float*; *flow*; *flounce*; *flop*. Coleridge himself uses some words of this group for their associative sound. Whether linguists agree or disagree that certain sounds rouse certain associations in the speaker's or listener's mind is immaterial. What matters is that Coleridge believed they did and that they did for him. Clearly, he disliked the sound of his own name, and his choice of such a fantastic *alias* was deliberate.

Coleridge was equally fascinated by word association. Early in his life he was an admirer of the psychologist/philosopher, David Hartley, as too was Wordsworth. Coleridge called his first son David Hartley. Much of Hartley's work was concerned with association. He extended to senses other than sight the idea, expressed in Newton's *Opticks* (1704), that the stimulus of light on the brain evoked predictable visual images.[2] Coleridge later rejected Hartley's determinism but retained his belief in the association of words. In *Biographia Literaria* he says:

Seeing a mackerel it may happen that I immediately think of gooseberries because I at the same time ate mackerel with gooseberries as the sauce. The first syllable of the latter word being that which had co-existed with the image of the bird so called, I may then think of a goose. In the next moment the image of a swan may arise before me, though I had never seen the two birds together.   (*BL*, VIII, p. 72)

Association in language, especially of words and sounds, is particularly important in Coleridge's best known poems, *The Ancyent Marinere*, *Kubla Khan* and *Christabel*.

Kubla Khan

The best remembered opening lines in all Coleridge's poems come in *Kubla Khan*:

> In Xanadu did Kubla Khan
> A stately pleasure-dome decree.

Even at this early stage, the strangeness of sound of the proper names has a spell-binding and, consequently, memorable power over the reader. Few people, however, can go on to quote the lines following and it is in these that Coleridge's verbal magic really begins to assert itself:

> Where Alph, the sacred river, ran
> Through caverns measureless to man
> Down to a sunless sea.

The reader experiences a not easily identifiable thrill, a sort of tingling of the senses. The lines leave us groping after a meaning that eludes us. They make 'sense' but have no meaning that we can relate to any world with which we are familiar. It is, as Coleridge himself said when writing a review of Mrs Radcliffe's *Mysteries of Udolpho* in 1794, as if:

> the secret, which the reader thinks himself every instant on the point of penetrating, flies like a phantom before him, and eludes his eagerness . . .[3]

This gives a clue to one very potent influence on Coleridge, not only in *Kubla Khan* but in other poems, particularly *Christabel*.

The rest of *Kubla Khan* follows a similar pattern in which the reader seeks in vain for any coherent statement, although words, phrases and whole lines emerge and touch a correspondent nerve as if we were on the brink of some profound understanding. If it does not reach us through any ordinary meaning – and Coleridge alleged that he had written it in a dream – the elusive quality that stirs these feelings in us must be in the language itself. There are two basic ways in which Coleridge produces the magical effect: both the sounds and the words rouse certain responses in the reader through the process of association.

Alliteration and repetition of sounds not always in initial position are very evident in the opening lines. The sibilants and nasal 'm's and 'n's should be noted. The vowel sounds are almost all open,[4] apart from the diphthong in the first syllable of *sacred* and the close front vowel of the final word *sea*. The effect of this is hard to gauge but it may help to reinforce the sense of space conjured up in the phrase *measureless to man*. *Cavern*, a word which Coleridge uses more than once in this poem, as well as in others, has a protracted, almost echo-like effect that its near synonym *cave* has not. This is partly the result of the disyllable with the resonant, lingering sound of the final nasal consonant, but also partly the difference of the open vowel sound of the first syllable in contrast to the half-closed diphthong of the /eɪ/ in *cave*. *Measureless* also contributes to the echoes set up by the other words with its alliterative consonants, open vowel sounds and the repetition in the next line of the suffix *-less*. In *sunless* we have an unexpected element, which Coleridge introduces from time to time. Another example of this is the juxtaposition of *sunny* and *ice* later in the poem:

> It was a miracle of rare device,
> A sunny pleasure-dome with caves of ice!

Had Coleridge written the more likely *sunlit sea*, the emotive thrill would have been lessened. Consciously we may hardly be aware of the negative form of *sunless* but it evokes a completely different response from a positive form of the word. The river descends into some darkly imagined abyss. Later this feeling is made explicit with the introduction of the verb *sank* in the line:

And sank in tumult to a lifeless ocean.

The suffix -less occurs again. The mysteriousness of the un
known of the Gothick novel is present here, as elsewhere in the
poem. A similar thrill of something unknown is felt in the
entire phrase measureless to man. The idea of something beyond
man's control has always created a frisson of danger, especially
since the ideas contained in Newtonian physics became widely
known among the more educated.

J. P. Ward has noted that when Wordsworth's feelings are
deeply engaged with his subject there is a similar use of
associative sounds. These, too, are nasals and sibilants.[5] Ward
finds words containing the nasal sounds 'm'; 'n' and 'ng'/ŋ/ are
prominent in the most powerful and memorable passages, and
also words combining nasals and sibilants. He cites passages
containing such lines as:

> a sense sublime
> Of something far more deeply interfused.

Words with these sounds seem to occur when there is a fusion
of outer and inner worlds, the natural and the mental or
spiritual. Although not wholly subscribing to the idea of
associative sound – 'we do not need to invest particular sounds
such as 'm' and 's' with certain necessary areas of connotation to
which they will normally be attached'[6] – Ward says that
'Wordsworth was clearly aware of the making of poetry as to do
with the impregnation of material sound with meaning
inseparably'.[7] His argument culminates in the word motion, a
key word in Wordsworth's poetry, since movement of the
mental faculties is mirrored or even prompted by the at times
imperceptible movement in the world of nature. Again, this
word is frequent when deep feeling is being conveyed by the
poet as in the passage of the 'egg stealing' which ends with the
line:

And with what motion moved the clouds.[8]

There is a clear similarity here between Wordsworth's use of
nasals and sibilants and Coleridge's, although Ward contends

that Wordsworth's use is built up within his own poetry and confined to it. In the line:

Five miles meandering with a mazy motion

it is remarkable that the word *motion* also occurs. This line also rouses a thrill as does the phrase 'with ceaseless turmoil seething' and the lines:

A damsel with a dulcimer
In a vision once I saw.

All these, it will be seen, contain the same combination of sounds as Ward noted in Wordsworth's memorable passages. In the first line of the second quotation here the sound patterning is extremely complex: apart from their initial alliteration *damsel* and *dulcimer* contain the same consonants (with a very minor exception) arranged in reverse order:

A damsel with a dulcimer
  d mz l /   d ls m

In addition the two initial stressed vowels are both front vowels and the shift from the half open 'a' in *damsel* /æ/ to the more open 'u' in *dulcimer* /ʌ/ is also slight, so much so that northerners often confuse these sounds when spoken by southerners. Further, *dulcimer* and *once I saw* constitute a near-rhyme, which is picked up three lines further on in 'Singing of Mount Abora'. The total effect of the sounds is strangely stirring and disturbing. The syntax of these two lines is also worth examining. The first line is a thematically marked complement which is rarer in Coleridge than in Wordsworth, as is thematic marking generally. Coleridge's syntax frequently follows the normal S V C (A) pattern and the word order of this entire clause is unusual. The second line is further inverted so that the subject and verb come at the end. The overall effect is not simply to throw the complement into prominence and make it thematic, but to produce a completely convoluted statement that mirrors the dream-like quality of the poem.

How far Coleridge consciously and deliberately set about

rousing associations is impossible to say. Apart from sound, certain words and combinations of words can arouse predictable responses. These are even less easy to explain but it is their indefinable quality that gives them their peculiar power in *Kubla Khan*. Examples may be capable of explanation to some extent, as:

> A savage place! as holy and enchanted
> As e'er beneath a waning moon was haunted
> By woman wailing for her demon-lover!

Some of the words used here form what is called a 'lexical set': that is they are linked by belonging to the same semantic 'field' or area of meaning. In this case the semantic field is the supernatural. The words which belong to the set are: *enchanted*; *haunted*; *demon-lover*, and possibly *holy*. Because of our experience of the supernatural and words frequently related to it in literature, other words in these lines take on similar associations and are loosely linked to the central set: *savage*; *moon*; *wailing*. It happens that this particular lexical set was the one used by the Gothick novelists of the late eighteenth century and Coleridge's writing very much reflects the language of that period. This type of vocabulary is frequently found in the poetry of Gray and Collins. In addition Coleridge was influenced by his close acquaintance with folk lore and fairy tale. Both he and Wordsworth read the Arabian Nights as children and this group of stories combines fairy tale and the East.

The second line of the following quotation is another example:

> And 'mid this tumult Kubla heard from far
> Ancestral voices prophesying war!

This also rouses echoes of things that we cannot quite bring to the surface. Coleridge's language often refuses to submit to objective linguistic analysis and little work has been done on this psychological aspect of language. 'Ancestral voices' may be explained and defined grammatically, semantically or by its function but its essential effect cannot be explained in any of these ways. Combined with 'prophesying war' the words seem to reach down to some deep instinct, the long history of the need to defend the human race. Much of the ritual, the words and the music, of ceremonies such as Remembrance Day rely on similar associative responses. The associations roused by Coleridge's words, however, must in part, if not wholly, result from knowledge and experience.

Apart from the associative features of language, there are other things to note in *Kubla Khan*. Much of the vocabulary is exotic. Some is derived from words associated with the East or even, as in the names, of directly eastern origin. These may be found sporadically in other poems by Coleridge but for obvious reasons they are most conspicuous and dense in *Kubla Khan*. An interest in things eastern was again very much a preoccupation of the time and Coleridge was not alone in being fascinated by it. English ladies, Lady Mary Wortley Montagu and, later, Lady Hester Stanhope, the niece of the younger Pitt, both toured what we today call the Middle East. The oriental vocabulary, therefore, would have received a sympathetic and knowledgeable reading. Another aspect of the vocabulary is its 'Romantic' quality, which again connects it to the Gothick novels of the late eighteenth century. Words such as *chasm*; *cavern*; *tumult*; *turmoil*, and even *romantic* itself colour the whole of the poem. Because of this, more ordinary words like *hill*; *rocks*, and *river* take on a surrealistic quality very different from the naturalistic associations they carry in the poetry of Wordsworth and in some of Coleridge's other poems. The strangeness assumed by otherwise familiar words is enhanced by combination into groups or compound words, such as 'incense-bearing tree', the 'waning moon' collocating with *haunted*, 'forests ancient as the hills' and 'deep romantic chasm'. An unusual word is *cedarn* in 'cedarn cover'. One might be forgiven for thinking this was a coinage by Coleridge – his prose writings are full of coinages – but it had been used by Milton, whose influence on Coleridge's language, as well as on that of Wordsworth, was considerable. In spite of the fact that the vocabulary is unusual, either in itself or by its collocations, however, much of it is concrete and here, as elsewhere, Coleridge uses a large number of evocative adjectives. There are relatively few striking verbs. Most verbs are stative and this is scarcely surprising in a poem that is basically descriptive. Coleridge rarely relies on verbs to carry his meaning. In this he is close to Wordsworth. However, although Wordsworth uses verbs sparingly and even then they are often lexically empty, stative or copula verbs, they carry a weight out of proportion to their frequency and apparent meaning in a way that Coleridge's hardly ever do.

Metaphor, simile and, in his earlier poems, personification are Coleridge's stock in trade as far as figurative language is concerned, but in *Kubla Khan*, apart from grammatical metaphor inherent in all normal language, he confines himself to simile. Three similes come close together and of these only the first (p. 128), by reason of its supernatural overtones, seems to suit with the spirit of the poem.

One characteristic of Coleridge's sentences is his predilection for repeating words and phrases, sometimes more than once, within a few lines. This is another feature which we saw in Wordsworth's poems, especially those in ballad form. Various nominal groups are repeated in *Kubla Khan*: 'the sacred river' occurs three times; 'caverns measureless to man' twice, and various combinations of 'sunny pleasure-dome' and 'caves of ice', as well as single words. The accumulations in this poem contribute to its atmosphere. In other poems Coleridge uses this device of repetition for other ends.

Overall, the language of *Kubla Khan*, a poem unlike any other in English, evokes the magical quality of a dream. Yet Coleridge said that he could 'not write without a *body* of *thought*' (*Letters*, I, 137). George Sampson notes that 'Of all the poems in the English language, the best parts of *The Ancient Mariner*, and the whole of *Kubla Khan* and *Christabel* are most free from "a body of thought"'.[9]

The 'Conversation' Poems

Coleridge wrote several fine blank verse poems, sometimes known as 'conversation' poems, that are almost lyrical in quality. Among these are 'The Eolian Harp', 'Fears in Solitude', 'Frost at Midnight', 'The Nightingale' and 'This Lime-Tree Bower My Prison'. Those named here have certain linguistic features in common and all, except the first, owe something to Wordsworth, and almost certainly to Dorothy.

'The Eolian Harp' appeared in *Poems* of 1796 under the title 'Effusion xxxv'. The manuscript is dated 20 August 1795, which means it was written about the time that Wordsworth and Coleridge first met. It can scarcely, therefore, have been influenced by Wordsworth at all. In spite of this the title and the entire 'message' of the poem reflect the 'wise passiveness', the 'negative capability' that was to become the essence of Wordsworth's thinking. It was not until 1817, when it appeared in *Sybilline Leaves* (1817), that Coleridge changed the title to 'The Eolian Harp'. The harp, which appears first as a 'Lute', purports to be part of the actual setting of the poem, and later becomes, in Coleridge's speculations, the 'organic Harps' of 'animated nature'. This type of instrument, which is referred to in Greek legend,[10] is hung up in the open air and the notes are drawn from the strings by the winds. It is, therefore, a 'passive' instrument in human terms, since it is activated at random by a natural force and not by deliberate human intent. The second reference to it carries several of the hallmarks of Wordsworth's language as it appears in *The Prelude*:

> And what if all of animated nature
> Be but organic Harps diversely fram'd
> That tremble into thought, as o'er them sweeps
> Plastic and vast, one intellectual breeze
> At once the Soul of each, and God of all?

The subjects of the two clauses, *animated nature* and *one intellectual breeze*, not only recall Wordsworth's particular vocabulary but could easily be found in similar functions in his poetry. The second is the actor as well as the subject of its clause, a type of inanimate actor which was commonly used by Wordsworth.

In the preceding paragraph Coleridge draws a picture of himself in a state of passivity. The line:

> And tranquil muse upon tranquillity

foreshadows Wordsworth's 'emotion recollected in tranquillity'. This short section (10 lines) seems, however, disjointed and almost disconnected from the opening of the poem. Here we come on one of the differences between Coleridge's poetry and

Wordsworth's. Most of Coleridge's blank verse poems open
with a description of the setting, which evokes certain thoughts
in the poet/narrator. From this point, however, he frequently
takes off in an unpredictable fashion, his mind flitting from
subject to subject. His manner of writing is summed up in some
lines from this poem:

> Full many a thought uncall'd and undetain'd,
> And many idle flitting phantasies,
> Traverse my indolent and passive brain,
> As wild and various as the random gales
> That swell and flutter on this subject Lute!

Here, the word *subject* means that the lute is subject to the
whims of the breeze. In the same way the poet is subject to
thoughts, or 'phantasies' as he calls them, which come not of his
own volition. Within the context of the poem, of course, this
passage has its own coherence but it is, nevertheless, indicative
of Coleridge's frequent inability to sustain a train of thought.

A characteristic of Coleridge's language, both vocabulary
and, to some extent, syntax, is its diversity and this makes
generalisations about it difficult. In 'The Eolian Harp' this is
particularly clear. The poem begins with an idealised description of the scene outside the cottage where the poet and his
wife, Sara, are sitting at evening. Here, the natural objects, the
flowers, are simply named and are mere conventions. The
'white-flower'd Jasmin' and the 'broad-leav'd Myrtle' are immediately converted into symbols of 'Innocence and Love', as is
the evening star, which becomes an emblem for 'Wisdom'.
Coleridge had yet to learn to look at nature for itself. There
seems to be more realism in:

> How exquisite the scents
> Snatch'd from yon bean-field!

and also in the 'stilly murmur of the distant Sea'. These, too,
however, are ultimately little more than conventional observations.

After this commonplace and rather stilted opening, Coleridge
introduces the Lute, in a singularly unrealistic way:

> that simplest Lute,
> Placed length-ways in the clasping casement . . .

The use of the participial adjective in *the clasping casement*, with its human connotations, reads very oddly. Coleridge then plunges into one of his 'magical' passages and the vocabulary changes to accommodate words suitable to the register of Fairyland. In these lines he uses his gift for evoking musical sounds as in *Kubla Khan*. The sibilant 's' and 'f' sounds of the lines:

> the long sequacious notes
> Over delicious surges sink and rise,
> Such a soft floating witchery of sound
> As twilight Elfins make

evoke the magical quality of the music even though they lack the particular thrill of the sounds of *Kubla Khan*. The introduction of the adjective *sequacious*, which, from its Latinate origin, at first seems out of keeping with the rest of the vocabulary, is bold but effective. Its sibilants match those in the rest of the words, and the cloying 'qu' /kw/, which is picked up in the verb *sink*, adds to the effect indicated by the word *honey-dropping*, not itself mimetic, which occurs a little later. This section is full of similes which themselves create the magic world conjured up by the sound of the lute.

Not only in its subject matter but also in its use of language, this magical interlude is far removed from the reality of emotion that Wordsworth would have written about. The final lines, reverting once more to the emblematic in the personification of music, are typical of the eighteenth century, although, again, not the eighteenth-century style that Wordsworth followed in his early poems in couplets:

> and the mute still air
> Is Music slumbering on her instrument.

Here the conceit and the language in which it is expressed are very much in the style of Gray or Collins. This sudden switch of style is accounted for by the fact that Coleridge added the final eight lines of this paragraph some years after the rest of the poem was composed.[11] The next two short verse paragraphs contain the Wordsworthian ideas already noted and reinforce the startling shifts of Coleridge's approach to his subject matter and the language in which he expresses it. The final paragraph, too, with its direct address to Sara, recalls the way in which Wordsworth addresses Dorothy in 'Tintern Abbey', although that poem was written some three years later. The use of negatives to express a positive proposition is also typical of Wordsworth, although Wordsworth's negatives do not draw attention to themselves in the way Coleridge's do by their obtrusive contortedness:

> nor such thoughts
> Dim and unhallow'd dost thou not reject.

With Coleridge this is a favourite method of using negatives. Another example occurs in 'This Lime-Tree Bower My Prison':

> Nor in this bower,
> This little lime-tree bower, have I not mark'd
> Much that has sooth'd me.

The final emphasis placed on the word *feels* in 'The Eolian Harp':

> with Faith that inly *feels*

is, however, wholly typical of Wordsworth, both in its emotional content (a common inheritance of the late eighteenth century) and in its absolute and emphatic use of the word without any elaboration.

This poem exemplifies the essential impulse behind Coleridge's poetic and linguistic habits: his almost inconsequential jumping from one subject to another with its concomitant shift in the type of language, especially vocabulary. In the later blank verse poems there is frequently a more sustained attempt to describe the setting realistically with the attention to detail that he may well have learned from either William or Dorothy. Those details which Wordsworth deliberately excluded from his own descriptions, even to the extent of cutting them out in revisions, mark a different approach and poetic development in the two men. Apart from this growth in his power to describe natural phenomena, Coleridge already in his early poems paid an attention to certain details, such as sound, and possessed a sometimes delicate, sometimes robust, manner of conjuring up immediate atmosphere that is not always present in Wordsworth's poetry. In contrast to Wordsworth's evocation of feelings, sensations and events that are past, Coleridge tries to extract every drop of emotion from the present moment. The particular conception aroused by the phrase 'kept his eye on the object' that has erroneously come down to us associated with Wordsworth belongs more truly to Coleridge. Wordsworth's own assertion in the 1800 Preface that he 'endeavoured to look steadily at [his] *subject*' [My italics] (*LB*, p. 251) is certainly true and something that Coleridge often failed to do. These variations of the one phrase are useful touchstones for the understanding of what each poet was attempting to do, or at least succeeded in doing.

In 'Fears in Solitude' (1798), Coleridge follows his usual pattern. He describes the place in which he is or imagines the poem to be set:

> The hills are heathy, save that swelling slope,
> Which hath a gay and gorgeous covering on,
> All golden with the never-bloomless furze,
> Which now blooms most profusely.

Here, adjectives proliferate, and the three describing the furze also alliterate. In addition there is the repetition of *bloom* in two different forms: *bloomless*, a negatively expressed adjective, and *blooms* a verb. Coleridge then describes the dell lying in the hollow of this upland landscape:

> but the dell,
> Bathed by the mist, is fresh and delicate
> As vernal corn-field, or the unripe flax,
> When, through its half-transparent stalks, at eve,
> The level sunshine glimmers with green light.

In these lines, Coleridge moves into one of his detailed similes and, as so often, it takes over, so that the description of the evening light, seen through the stalks of the flax, is itself executed with extreme precision and care. In the process, however, one looses the sense of the grassy hollow. The transference of the simile to any visual image of the dell is awkward. Even within the simile itself there is almost an over-precision. Coleridge often conveys the impression of striving after effect.

Coleridge was clearly fascinated by the effects of light and shade and in 'This Lime-Tree Bower' the descriptions are rather more telling because they are linked directly to the objects being described. Of the various descriptions of this kind, one of the most effective is of the leaves of the tree above him in the 'bower' as the poet contemplates them:

> Pale beneath the blaze
> Hung the transparent foliage; and I watch'd
> Some broad and sunny leaf, and lov'd to see
> The shadow of the leaf and stem above
> Dappling its sunshine!

The final two lines, which accurately convey a picture of the shadow of one leaf seen through another, contain no adjectives at all. 'Dappling its sunshine', the climax of the image, consists of a verb in participial form and a noun. However, there is no doubt that these words would not be effective without the preceding adjectives *transparent* and *broad*, which conjure up a general picture of the leaves of the tree. Even so, the visual impact is not immediate; only a careful and close reading will yield the picture that the poet seeks to draw.

Another example of Coleridge's precise visual perception is the description of the fire in 'Frost at Midnight':

> the thin blue flame
> Lies on my low-burnt fire, and quivers not;
> Only that film, which fluttered on the grate,
> Still flutters there, the sole unquiet thing.

Again, Coleridge relies very much on adjectives, with five in four lines. The repetition of *flutter*, this time in variant forms of the verb, should also be noticed.

All these descriptive vignettes are achieved with basically concrete and simple vocabulary. Here again the language of Wordsworth and Coleridge shows evidence of a common source. *Leaf*; *stem*; *fire*; *grate*; *stalks*; *sunlight* are all everyday nouns. The adjectives, too, are for the most part common enough, including a number of colour words, and are generally of native stock. *Transparent*, used in two descriptions, is an imported word but only the very unusual *sequacious* from 'The Eolian Harp' shows any great daring in usage. Verbs, too, are basic although often mimetic: suggestive of movement, as *flutters*, or of sight and movement, as *glimmers* and *dappling*. On the whole, there are relatively few verbs but those used are striking and contain this mimetic quality. They are verbs which play upon the senses. The beginning of 'Frost at Midnight' is somewhat different in that the description (a statement rather than a description perhaps) does not rely on adjectives and the words are more abstract. In the way it conjures up an impression of frost, however, it is quite as effective as any of the more pictorial descriptions that Coleridge draws:

> The Frost performs its secret ministry,
> Unhelped by any wind.

There are only six lexically full words in this brief one-and-a-half line evocation of the frost, and in the first line, apart from the word *frost* itself, the three telling words, one verb, one adjective and one noun, are more elevated and literary than the vocabulary in the short passages looked at so far. Yet who could deny that the impression of a frosty night is any less vivid? Admittedly, the second half line, with its down-to-earth *unhelped* and *wind*, contributes to the overall effect of stillness in which frost habitually descends; but it is the impact of the first line that arouses a thrill akin to the sensations felt in parts of *Kubla Khan*. This type of descriptive evocation is rare in Coleridge's poetry but the short opening to this poem demonstrates his at times perfect mastery of material. The sentence is both simple and short. The subject/actor of the statement is again an inanimate natural element and the idea of *ministry* associated with the forces of nature indicates the

Wordsworthian idea that nature ministers to the human mind. The collocation with *secret* indicates that the action is not only silent but unobserved by the human beings for whose benefit it works.

Later, Coleridge returns to more domestic and concrete detail. In the final verse paragraph the detail of a winter morning is again described in realistic terms:

> Whether...
> the redbreast sit and sing
> Betwixt the tufts of snow on the bare branch
> Of mossy apple-trees, while the nigh thatch
> Smokes in the sun-thaw.

The final clause is especially vivid and shows that Coleridge is at his best when he does not rely on adjectives for description. The verb *smokes* and the compound *sun-thaw* (which by its compression avoids the use of an adjective) catches an image of the thatch steaming in the morning sun in half a dozen words. At the close, Coleridge brings back the exact wording of the opening line of the poem: 'the secret ministry of frost' and it is again the actor of the final clause of the poem:

> the secret ministry of frost
> Shall hang them up in silent icicles,
> Quietly shining to the quiet Moon.

The repetition of the opening is resolved in the final line, a postmodifier of *icicles*. Coleridge uses his particular type of close repetition of a word in different grammatical forms with *quiet* first as an adverb and then as an adjective. These two words, followed by the long vowel and nasal consonants of *moon*, encapsulate the atmosphere that pervades the whole poem: a seeming extension of the present moment into past and future.

A similar repetition, although this time the words are both verbs and identical, occurs in the description of the ash in 'This Lime-Tree Bower':

> whose few poor yellow leaves
Ne'er tremble in the gale, yet tremble still,
Fann'd by the water-fall!

The tree is so sheltered that its leaves are not reached by the wind and only the slight disturbance of air caused by the falling water makes them move as if in a breeze. The extended description of this secluded dell is less strained than that of the hollow in 'Fears In Solitude'. Once more, adjectives occur in profusion and there is a brief simile attached to the tree, 'Its slim trunk ... arching like a bridge'. But the precision of the leaves trembling in the motion of the waterfall does not rely on adjectives. The description with the weeds by the water's brim:

> the dark green file of long lank weeds,
That all at once (a most fantastic sight!)
Still nod and drip beneath the dripping edge
Of the blue clay-stone.

Coleridge seems singularly fascinated by this combination of words for he used it earlier in his play *Osorio*, which was written by March 1797. A revised version under the title of *Remorse* was printed in 1813, when it was staged at Drury Lane. The variant of the lines quoted above appears in Act IV:

> a jutting clay-stone,
Drops on the long lank weed, that grows beneath:
And the weed nods and drips.   (*Remorse* IV, i, 17–19)

The same combination of adjectives occurs even earlier in the poem 'Melancholy', published, according to Coleridge, in 1794. Describing the 'dark green Adder's Tongue', Coleridge writes of its 'long lank leaf'. One may well wonder if these early uses of *long* in combination with *lank* prompted Wordsworth to finish the nominal group 'long lank slips' of currants in 'The Ruined Cottage' in this way, the completion of which eluded him for so long (p. 65, n. 2).

In spite of the attention to precise detail Coleridge paid in many of his poems, much of his language is general, although not in the same way as Wordsworth's. For instance, after setting the scene in 'Fears in Solitude', he continues:

> Oh! 'tis a quiet spirit-healing nook!
> Which all, methinks, would love; but chiefly he
> The humble man, who in his youthful years,
> Knew just so much of folly, as has made
> His early manhood more securely wise!

Wordsworth only rarely alludes simply to someone as indefinite as 'the humble man', using the representative definite article *the*. This is a typical eighteenth-century mode of expression. Wordsworth's 'humble man' would have been a Leech-gatherer or a Shepherd or even a 'discharged Soldier'. When Wordsworth uses generalised language it is in quite a different way and for a different reason.[12]

Coleridge used other types of generalised expression and abstract vocabulary. Whereas many of Wordsworth's abstract words are those denoting emotions or qualities, Coleridge, although he has a sprinkling of these, has a much wider range of general words. In 'Fears in Solitude', for instance, once he has left the natural scene that sets his thoughts in motion, he moves into a tirade against English oppression and thence to the unreliability of men's words and their hypocrisy. Fear of imminent invasion is left far behind at this point. In this section Coleridge introduces long lists of words of the following type:

> at home,
> All individual dignity and power
> Engulfed in Courts, Committees, Institutions,
> Associations and Societies. . . .
> We have drunk up, demure as at a grace.

The individual is quite deliberately obliterated by the facelessness of society's institutions. Note also the metaphor in the last line and the simile contained within it. Both are far removed from the world of nature and are part of an institutionalised society. The picture presented is of an urban world. The whole passage is, of course, metaphorical and in an urbane, eighteenth-century style. This type of diction contrasts vividly with that which Coleridge uses in his natural descriptions and also with the mystic and ethereal language he used in the extended 'elfin' simile in the 'Eolian Harp' or the vocabulary of the sublime in *Kubla Khan*.

Different again is another area of vocabulary in 'Fears in Solitude'. In those parts of the poem where Coleridge deals with the subject intimated in the gloss to the title, 'the alarm of an invasion', the vocabulary is full of words related to war which are similarly abstract and general:

> What uproar and what strife may now be stirring
> This way or that o'er these silent hills –
> Invasion, and the thunder and the shout,
> And all the crash of onset; fear and rage,
> And undetermined conflict –

Other words of the same lexical set, including the word *war* itself, are: *carnage*; *bloodshed*; *battle*; *siege*; *famine*; *pestilence*; *plague*. These are nearer to the type of nouns found in Wordsworth's 'The Female Vagrant' but Coleridge uses them in a more rhetorical manner and does not relate them to the business of war *per se*. Typical of his use are such lines as:

> A groan of accusation pierces Heaven!

and:

> No speculation on contingency,
> However dim and vague, too vague and dim
> To yield a justifying cause....

In the second line of the second quotation Coleridge also uses the device of repeating identical words but in reverse order.

The same types of generalities in the language, abstract vocabulary and occasional instances of strain or uneven usage, can be found in most of the 'conversation' poems. The one possible exception is 'Frost at Midnight', where Coleridge sustains one level throughout. This poem is a particularly good example of his use of word association. It depends very much on the principle of association, and the way in which the ideas are connected is more easily traceable in this poem than in most. The apparently odd jumps that Coleridge seems to make on occasions form a sequence of linked thoughts here. Particularly clear is the image of the smoky film which flutters on the fire and reminds him of how he watched the same phenomenon when at school:

> Presageful, have I gazed upon the bars,
> To watch that fluttering *stranger*!

The italics are Coleridge's, and he picks up the word some lines further on when the opening door of the schoolroom makes his heart leap in expectation of seeing the stranger augured by the fluttering film.[13] This passage about his own schooldays, which leads naturally on from the contemplation of his sleeping infant son by way of the connecting object, the fire, serves to show the loneliness of his own childhood. This in turn moves forward to the different life he foresees for his son, who is to be brought up in the countryside. Here, Coleridge again uses repeated words:

> By lakes and sandy shores, beneath the crags
> Of ancient mountain, and beneath the clouds,
> Which image in their bulk both lakes and shores
> And mountain crags.

The repetition here has a more definable function in that the formation of the clouds in the sky reflects the scenes of nature below. This is an unusual inversion of the more expectable reflection of the sky in the waters of the lake. Finally the re-introduction of the frost, which itself is part of the natural world the sleeping child is to live in and love, brings the poem full circle. The return to the opening scene of a poem – the poetic equivalent of the musical *rondo* – is a favourite device in these lyrical blank verse poems but in none does it occur more naturally or inevitably than in 'Frost at Midnight'.

So far little has been said of Coleridge's syntax. His sentence structure is more straightforward than Wordsworth's and he usually starts a sentence with the subject followed immediately, or almost immediately, by the main verb. There is little of the separation of sentence elements such as we saw in Wordsworth's blank verse. The poems frequently start with short statements and also end with them. The openings of the poems in this section are frequently conversational, which is partly why they are called 'conversation' poems. The first sentence of 'This Lime-Tree Bower' is:

> Well, they are gone, and here I must remain,
> This lime-tree bower my prison!

Well is a typical gambit for opening a conversation. The use of the pronominal *they* with no previous referent, also makes it seem that the speaker is talking to someone who is beside him. As the poem progresses, however, we sense that the poet is addressing the reader or even possibly talking to himself. Following the initial statement in the first line, the second line is virtually an appended exclamation and this is also common in these poems. A longer opening, although it contains a similarly simple statement, is found in a poem not previously discussed, 'The Nightingale', which is actually subtitled 'A conversation poem'. This was published in the first edition of *Lyrical Ballads* (1798). The opening is more symmetrically arranged, two subjects preceding the verb and two following:

> No cloud, no relique of the sunken day
> Distinguishes the West, no long thin slip
> Of sullen light, no obscure trembling hues.

In spite of the apparent artifice of these three lines, the simplicity of the overall structure makes them acceptable in a conversational poem. Following this comes a line of a similar conversational nature to the one in 'This Lime-Tree Bower':

> Come, we will rest on this old mossy bridge!

Again, the poet appears to be addressing someone, both by reason of the quasi-imperative *Come* and by the inclusive pronoun *we*. Later, these persons are revealed as 'My Friend, and thou, our Sister!' – almost certainly Wordsworth and Dorothy. Although the conversational features are prominent throughout this poem, the reader has no sense of eavesdropping and feels more that the poet is addressing the people named through the medium of thought rather than directly in person. After the opening,'The Nightingale' continues in a series of apostrophes, common to all these poems. The short and relatively simple initial statements then lead into longer sentences, as Coleridge moves away from the settings to the thoughts they rouse. Here we can see another type of resumptive syntax, quite different from Wordsworth's. Coleridge frequently repeats a word from the opening lines, using it as a kind of bridge to the more speculative part of the poem. An example from 'The Nightingale' is the word *melancholy*, first associated with the nightingale of the title:

> And hark! the Nightingale begins its song,
> 'Most musical, most melancholy' bird!
> A melancholy bird? Oh! idle thought!
> In Nature there is nothing melancholy.

The short statement in the last line introduces the next theme of the poem and this is followed by a lengthy and generalised statement. On this occasion the subject, 'some night-wandering man', is modified so much that it has the appearance of using Wordsworth's syntactical device of separating the subject from the verb and, indeed, the subject has to be repeated before the verb with a pleonastic pronoun *he*, so far is the head, *man*, of the subject group left behind:

> But some night-wandering man whose heart was pierced
> With the remembrance of a grievous wrong,
> Or slow distemper, or neglected love
> (And so, poor wretch! filled all things with himself,
> And made all gentle sound tell back the tale
> Of his own sorrow) he, and such as he,
> First named these notes a melancholy strain.

This repetition of the subject is part of the conversational impression the sentence structure conveys. The poem continues in this way, short statements alternating with more lengthy complex ones, frequently picking up the thread of the argument by repeating a word from the previous sentence. Many of

Coleridge's sentences are exclamations and these frequently have no verb. There are occasionally other sentences without verbs, and these are known as presentative sentences. It is as if something were simply held out to the reader for his inspection and nothing predicated about it. Usually Coleridge's sentences of this type are combined with exclamation, as in the following from 'Frost at Midnight':

> Sea, hill, and wood,
> This populous village! Sea, and hill, and wood,
> With all the numberless goings-on of life
> Inaudible as dreams!

The first of these sentences is perhaps the more typical; the second, with its lengthy trailing prepositional phrase has almost the effect of a predication, although without any verb. 'The Eolian Harp' has more sentences of this type than the other 'conversation' poems. One example is:

> O! the one Life within us and abroad,
> Which meets all motion and becomes its soul,
> A light in sound, a sound-like power in light,
> Rhythm in all thought, and joyance everywhere.

The first two lines, which include a relative clause, form a typically Coleridgean presentative sentence. The four short nominal groups following the word *soul* are in effect four presentative clauses. The first two show Coleridge's fondness for verbal repetition, again with the order reversed.

Wordsworth's underlying sentence structure is not predominantly of the subordinate kind, in spite of the length of some of his sentences. If anything, Coleridge's style is even less subordinate; his sentence structures are basically co-ordinate, although he also has, at times, long clauses. Typical of his style is this passage from the end of 'This Lime-Tree Bower':

> Pale beneath the blaze
> Hung the transparent foliage; and I watch'd
> Some broad and sunny leaf, and lov'd to see
> The shadow of the leaf and stem above

Dappling its sunshine! And that walnut-tree
Was richly ting'd, and a deep radiance lay
Full on the ancient ivy, which usurps
Those fronting elms, and now, with blackest mass
Makes dark branches gleam a lighter hue
Through the late twilight: and although now the bat
Wheels silent by, and not a swallow twitters,
Yet still the solitary humble-bee
Sings in the bean-flower!

Here are seven quite short co-ordinate clauses in eleven whole
and two half lines, and two more within a subordinate clause.
There are only two subordinating conjunctions, one a relative
and the second, beginning with *though*, containing the two
further co-ordinate clauses. Even the number of prepositional
phrases (a feature of Wordsworth's long clauses) is slight.
There are four altogether and two of these contain only the
preposition and an unmodified noun (apart from an article)
while the other two have one premodifying adjective each,
'through the late twilight' and 'with blackest mass'. The use of
the co-ordinating conjunctions *and* and *but*, particularly *and*, to
start a sentence also occurs here and Coleridge frequently
begins both sentences and verse paragraphs in this way. This is
another means by which the conversational style is achieved.

Not all of Coleridge's clauses are as short as in the example
just given and they tend to be shorter in the descriptive
passages at the beginning and end of the poems and longer in
the more meditative sections in between. How does Coleridge
lengthen his clauses and sentences if not by subordination?
One very frequent way is through his use of figurative language.
Very often a sentence is lengthened by the introduction of a
simile. Some of these are short but in others Coleridge gets
carried away into a long and circumstantial development of the
thing used for comparison, even to the extent of bringing in
further similes, as in this example from 'Fears in Solitude':

As if a Government had been a robe,
On which our vice and wretchedness were tagged
Like fancy-points and fringes, with the robe
Pulled off at pleasure.

Others, although short, follow in rapid succession, as the following two from 'The Nightingale':

> and these wakeful birds
> Have all burst forth in choral minstrelsy,
> As if some sudden gale had swept at once
> A hundred airy harps!

The aeolian harp is a persistent image in these poems. Just
four lines later the song of a single nightingale is compared to
'tipsy Joy that reels with tossing head.' Coleridge does not
wholly avoid subordinate clauses and these often enter into the
longer similes as well as other parts of the poem. He also uses
participial clauses, although not often, and also appositive lists.
One was quoted earlier from 'Fears in Solitude'. This poem has
a particularly large number of such lists. Another example is:

> To me, who from thy lakes and mountain-hills,
> Thy clouds, thy quiet dales, thy rocks and seas,
> Have drunk in all my intellectual life,
> All sweet sensations, all ennobling thoughts,
> All adoration of the God in nature,
> All lovely and honourable things. . . .

There are two lists here: the first gives the natural objects
which have afforded the assimilation of the emotional and
spiritual sensations, and the sensations follow.

Coleridge's sentences and clauses, while frequently short and
uncomplicated and essentially co-ordinate, are very varied in
structure. This gives his poetry vitality. The conversational
quality of the blank verse poems is maintained partly by this
variety but mainly through the co-ordination and the various
conversational openings and resumptions, by the use of direct
address and the pronouns associated with it: *you* and particularly
we. He is thus able to carry the reader along with him through
sometimes unexpected twists of thought and argument.

Christabel and *The Ancyent Marinere*

When Wordsworth and Coleridge planned to write a volume of
poems together in 1797–8, they decided 'that a series of poems
might be composed of two sorts. In one the incidents and
agents were to be, in part, at least supernatural' (*BL*, II,
p. 5). It fell to Coleridge to write these poems about 'persons
and characters supernatural, or at least romantic'. *The Rime of
the Ancyent Marinere* was the chief of these and was the first
poem in the first edition of *Lyrical Ballads*. *Christabel* was to have
appeared in the second edition of 1800 but Wordsworth
countermanded the printing of it, substituting further poems
of his own. Part I of *Christabel* was written in 1797, about the
same time as *The Ancyent Marinere*, and Part II was added in
1800. But the poem was not printed, even in this unfinished
state, until 1816.

Although both *The Ancyent Marinere* and *Christabel* have their
genesis in the traditional-type poems found in Percy's *Reliques*
and other antiquarian collections, only the supernatural element
really links them. Whereas *The Ancyent Marinere* is essentially a
pastiche in traditional ballad style, *Christabel* is a historically-
based metrical romance, having more in common with
Wordsworth's 'Hart-Leap Well' and 'The White Doe of
Rylstone'. It also owes something to the Gothick novels which
Coleridge was reading in his early twenties.

Coleridge's nephew, Henry Nelson Coleridge, referred to
Christabel as 'the thing ... the most difficult of execution in the
whole field of romance – witchery by daylight – and the success
is complete'.[14] In spite of a certain unevenness, mainly in
expression, which is typical of Coleridge, *Christabel* justifie
this assessment. The music of the lines is an integral part of the
poem's magic. This is most evident in the short descriptions of
which Coleridge is a master. The stillness of night at the
opening of the poem is conveyed partly through negatives. The
absence of wind is expressed in two parallel clauses that juxtapose the beauty of Christabel with the late winter landscape:

There is not wind enough in the air
To move away the ringlet curl
From the lovely lady's cheek –

> There is not wind enough to twirl
> The one red leaf, the last of its clan,
> That dances as often as dance it can,
> Hanging so light, and hanging so high,
> On the topmost twig that looks up at the sky.

The detail of the leaf comes from Dorothy Wordsworth's *Journal* for 7 March 1798: 'One only leaf upon the top of a tree – the sole surviving leaf – danced round and round like a rag blown by the wind' (I, 11–12). Coleridge is carried away by the image he sees in his mind's eye rather than by what is suited to the context: the leaf appears to dance whereas it should be still in the windless night. These two clauses contain several characteristic features of Coleridge's language. The first line of each clause is repeated almost exactly and in the second clause there is repetition of the verbs *dance(s)* and *hanging*. Alliteration is present in 'lovely lady', 'hanging so high' and 'topmost twig', and repetition of vowel sounds in the words *light* and *high*, as well as the rhyming word *sky*, contributes to the impression of the leaf dancing. The two short clauses, 'hanging so light, and hanging so high', consist mainly of unvoiced consonants, including three aspirate 'h's. These, together with the slight upward glide of the diphthongs /aɪ/ and the mimetic swinging effect of the nasal 'ng' /ŋ/ sounds, conjure up a vivid picture of the leaf. There is also the typical Coleridgean touch of colour in '*red leaf*', which does not occur in Dorothy's *Journal* entry.

There is nothing particularly sinister in this description. Earlier the setting has contained ominous hints:

> The night is chilly, but not dark.
> The thin gray cloud is spread on high,
> It covers but not hides the sky.
> The moon is behind, and at the full;
> And yet she looks both small and dull.
> The night is chill, the cloud is gray:
> 'Tis a month before the month of May,
> And the Spring comes slowly up this way.

This description, too, is found in Dorothy's *Journal*, for 31 January 1798: 'Set forward to Stowey at half-past five. When we left home the moon immensely large, the sky scattered over with clouds. These soon closed in, contracting the dimensions of the moon without concealing her' (I, 5). The contrast between the actual condition of the moon and its appearance, coupled with the half-concealment of the sky by the 'thin gray cloud' presents an image of a night that is both light and dark, a disconcerting ambivalence that is to be reiterated throughout the poem. The final clause, joined by *and*, as if it had an additional significance on this occasion: 'and moreover' or 'and don't forget', brings out the strangeness of the preceding lines. The rejuvenating force of the normal cycle of the seasons is disrupted.

These two quotations show the essential features of both the vocabulary and syntax of the poem. The setting of *Christabel* is concrete as far as vocabulary goes. There is no magic 'elfin' quality here. The vocabulary is normal and everyday, even colloquial in a phrase such as 'up this way', and largely monosyllabic. The clauses are short and either joined without any conjunctions (paratactic) or by the co-ordinating conjunctions *and* and *but*. In the earlier quotation the clauses were longer but basically simple in structure. They consist of two identically patterned existential *There* clauses with an infinitive *to* clause. The complement of the infinitive clause is expanded in both with the second longer than the first. The first has only a prepositional phrase while the second has a relative clause, two very short participial clauses and a final prepositional phrase. Both passages are typical of the language of the poem.

The interior descriptions, particularly that of Christabel's bedchamber, are also minutely observed with touches of vivid detail. Coleridge frequently resorted to eighteenth-century diction but here he looks forward to the language of Keats, especially that of 'The Eve of St Agnes':

> The chamber carved so curiously,
> Carved with figures strange and sweet,
> All made out of the carver's brain,
> For a lady's chamber meet:
> The lamp with twofold silver chain
> Is fastened to an angel's feet.

The last two lines anticipate the minute attention paid to detail by the Pre-Raphaelites of the later nineteenth century.

Throughout the poem there are lexical sets, each serving a particular purpose. For convenience these must be separated but the groups frequently overlap. The first set consists of those words which are archaic or denote historical matters. These give the poem its historical colouring. Archaic words include, *damsel*; *ween*; *assay*; *amain*; *I wis*, and *meet* in the sense of 'fitting'. Archaic exclamations and phrases are 'wel-a-day!', 'woe is me!', 'in maiden wise' and the ballad-like 'words of high disdain'. Words denoting objects in the historical setting are *boon*; *tourney court*; *cincture* (also an ecclesiastical term), the *boss* of Sir Leoline's shield, the *brands* of the dying fire and the *rushes* that form the covering of Christabel's chamber floor. Words such as *chamber* and *shield*, used in conjunction with the others, build up the historical atmosphere. There is, too, the word *robe* and in collocation with it another word used in an earlier meaning, which could easily be passed over, or which, if noticed, could be misleading:

> There she sees a damsel bright,
> Drest in a silken robe of white,
> That shadowy in the moonlight shone:
> The neck that made that white robe wan,
> Her stately neck, and arms were bare.

Wan is used in its now obsolete sense of 'dark' (Old English black'): the white robe seems dull beside the dazzling white of Geraldine's neck and arms. Archaic occupations, such as bard and sacristan (still used in ecclesiastical circles), add to the historical setting. These archaic or historical words are not very obtrusive but there are enough of them to evoke a sense of times past. Such usage is quite different from that of Wordsworth in his historical poems, 'The White Doe', 'Hart-leap Well' and 'Song at the Feast of Brougham Castle'. Wordsworth rarely has recourse to archaisms, although at times he necessarily uses a word denoting an archaic object. On the whole he keeps to his usual type of vocabulary, slightly more literary than that which he uses for his 'modern' ballads but otherwise very similar.

Another important set of words in *Christabel* is religious. Some words may be called 'positive' and some 'negative', reflecting the conflict between good and evil in the poem. Amongst such words and phrases with 'positive' connotations are *angel*; *pray*; *Heaven*; *virtuous powers*; *guardian spirit*; *the Virgin all divine*. Religious exclamations which also have religious connotations are: 'Jesu Maria, shield her well!', which occurs twice, and 'Mary, mother, save me now!' These are also historical or archaic-sounding. Other words, such as *soul* and *ghost* are strictly indeterminate, being neither good nor bad, although in the context they seem to fall in with the 'negative' words, such as: *knell*; *sexton*; *shroud*; *death*; *death-note*, and even more negative in a Christian sense: *sin*; *unholy*, and *unblest*. All these have associations with death, which enhances the atmosphere of impending doom. It is this second group that, in contrast with the first, carries the sense of the supernatural and heightens the impression of the potential evil power of Geraldine.

This evil is hinted at through sentences that are broken off. One extreme example is the intimation of some foul and obscene deformity in Geraldine that lies beneath her white robes:

> Her silken robe, and inner vest,
> Dropt to her feet, and full in view,
> Behold! her bosom and half her side –
> A sight to dream of, not to tell!

which is followed by the prayer:

> O shield her! shield sweet Christabel![15]

The very fact that Christabel needs protection from something unstated adds to the feeling that forces of darkness surround her. As Christabel slumbers in Geraldine's arms something shameful or sinful is hinted at again but once more the statement is broken off. This type of understatement is more effective than any revelation could be.

Details of the narrative impinge on the language and imply the presence of the supernatural. One of these is the apparent collapse of Geraldine each time Christabel unwittingly appeals to the powers of goodness, as when she trims the lamp in her bedchamber. The lamp with its chain and angel's feet, 'swinging to and fro', beings to mind a church censer and the sight causes Geraldine to sink to the floor. Again, when she drinks the cordial made by Christabel's mother she falls into a strange visonary fit, in which she seems to be assailed by the dead woman:

> Why stares she with unsettled eye?
> Can she the bodiless dead espy?

There is another rather loosely bound lexical set in which all the words denote or are associated with unpleasant things or the natural order is overturned. This wide-ranging set includes the *howls* of Sir Leoline's mastiff and her *angry moan* when the two ladies pass her as she lies asleep, the *owlet's scritch*, the fact that nothing grows on the oak tree behind which Christabel finds Geraldine but *moss and rarest mistletoe*, as well as words such as *dim*; *dull*; *gloom*; *mourning*; *dread*; *malice*; *treacherous hate*; *doleful*, and many others. The alternation between purity and evil is brought out in juxtaposed phrases, such as 'Now in glimmer, and now in gloom', where the balance of similar syntactical frames and alliteration draws attention to the balanced forces of good and evil.

The evil and negative side of the romance is also conveyed through the syntax. In this poem Coleridge uses a larger number of negatives and negatively expressed clauses than usual. At the beginning of the poem the setting is described in negative terms, which continue. Objects which are positively described are in or yield to a negative state. In the bedchamber:

> The silver lamp burns dead and dim;

and in the fire in the hall:

> The brands were flat, the brands were dying.

The negative expressions are scattered throughout the poem and frequently occur with antithesis of light and dark. In the bedchamber:

> The moon shines dim in the open air,
> And not a moonbeam enters here.

Yet the carvings on the walls can still be seen. This is not what one expects. Total darkness would seem to be more in keeping with the atmosphere of evil and impending disaster. However, this is all part of the ambivalent nature of the poem, a sort of twilight world in which reality is elusive.

Ambivalence is also conveyed by a metre not used by Coleridge elsewhere. He commented on this in the Preface of 1816, when the poem was first published:

> the metre of the Christabel is not, properly speaking, irregular, though it may seem so from its being founded on a new principle: namely, that of counting in each line the accent, not the syllables. The latter may vary from seven to twelve, yet in each line the accents will be found to be only four. Nevertheless, this occasional variation in number of syllables is not introduced wantonly, or for the mere ends of convenience, but in correspondence with some transition, in the nature of the imagery or passion.[16]

Occasionally there are not as many as four stresses in a line nor even seven syllables. However, these remarks on the stressed rather than the syllabic line make it clear that Coleridge was experimenting, and in two ways: firstly for the sake of an image – this can be seen at its most telling in the lines about the single leaf tossing in the wind, and secondly for the sake of transitions in 'passion' or feeling. The rhyme scheme is also irregular at times. The poem is mostly composed in couplets but sometimes the lines rhyme abab and occasionally the rhyming word is three lines further on. Irregularity of both metre and rhyme-scheme contribute to the sense of unease the poem generates. The role of Geraldine is itself equivocal: she is undoubtedly intended to be the agent of Christabel's destruction, but at times she seems to be herself the unwilling instrument of an evil power. The irregularity of the line lengths, apart from occurring in conjunction with certain imagery, frequently comes at points in the poem when Geraldine is allowing herself to be mastered by her evil fate. It is in these parts that 'passion' is at its most threatening. After an inward struggle, one of several, Geraldine yields to her evil role and takes her place beside Christabel on the bed:

> And in her arms the maid she took,
>   Ah wel-a-day!
> And with low voice and doleful look
>   These words did say:
> 'In the touch of this bosom there worketh a spell,
> Which is lord of thy utterance, Christabel!
> Thou knowest to-night, and wilt know to-morrow
> This mark of my shame, this seal of my sorrow;
>   But vainly thou warrest,
>   For this is alone in
>   Thy power to declare,
>   That in the dim forest
>   Thou heard'st a low moaning.
> And found'st a bright lady, surpassingly fair:
> And didst bring her home with thee in love and in charity,
> To shield her and shelter her from the damp air.'

This is the most sustained and the longest instance of metrical irregularity but there are others.

While he was beginning *Christabel*, Coleridge started writing *The Ancyent Marinere*. Whereas he finished *The Ancyent Marinere* in some six months, *Christabel* remained one of Coleridge's many fragments. Why did Coleridge manage to finish the one poem and not the other? Both share a background in tales of the supernatural and have certain features of language in common. The answer lies at least partly in the language and how it is deployed in the two poems.

All the features of Coleridge's language already noted are present in *The Ancyent Marinere* – concrete vocabulary, a large number of adjectives, including many colour adjectives, and short paratactic or co-ordinate clauses. There are perhaps even more short similes than usual and, as in *Christabel*, there are lexical sets, some of which they share because the subject matter is partially similar. There is one set denoting things of religious and Christian significance and another, related to it, to do with the supernatural. Apart from these, there are in *The*

Ancyent Marinere other sets connected with the topographical setting, the elements, which play a large part in the narrative, and the sea and sailing. The first version of the poem, published in *Lyrical Ballads* of 1798, also included a sprinkling of archaisms and old-fashioned spellings, words such as *Pheere* (this is found in the ballad of 'Sir Cauline' in Percy's *Reliques*); *eftsoons*, and *eldritch*; spellings such as *cauld* and *ancyent* and old plurals like *een* or archaic forms like *ne . . . ne*. These were intended to give an antiquarian air to the poem, but most of them were replaced in the second edition of 1800, probably at the suggestion of Wordsworth. The archaic form of constructing the past tense with *did*, as in 'The Ice did split', however, was retained. This may have come from the travel journals which Coleridge drew on extensively. Many of these were written earlier and have this older form.

There is a fundamental difference in the way in which the supernatural language is distributed in *The Ancyent Marinere* and in *Christabel*. In *Christabel* not only the historical and Romantic vocabulary but also hints of the supernatural set the poem at a remove from everyday life from the start. Unutterable horrors are left unstated in unfinished clauses. In addition, the enigmatic role of Geraldine is hinted at but not explained. The atmosphere is built up in such a way that any statement of the exact nature of the evil would come as an anticlimax. Perhaps Coleridge was aware of this. Perhaps he did not know what the ultimate horror was to be, although he protested that he did. In the 'Preface' of 1816 he wrote:

> . . . as, in my very first conception of the tale, I had the whole present to my mind, with the wholeness, no less than with the liveliness of a vision; I trust that I shall be able to embody in verse the three parts yet to come, in the course of the present year.[16]

In *The Ancyent Marinere* Coleridge set about relating his tale in a very different way. Two aspects of the language only will be examined here: the linguistic influence of the many travel journals Coleridge had read and the influence of the traditional ballad style. There were many contributory factors to Coleridge's language, such as his interest in science and other aspects of his wide reading, as well as his correspondence with Dorothy Wordsworth and entries in her *Journal.*

Even if Livingstone Lowes had not done such thorough research into Coleridge's reading,[17] the 'Argument' at the beginning of the poem might have given a clue to the probable source of Coleridge's expression and vocabulary:

> How a Ship having passed the Line was driven by Storms to the cold Country towards the South Pole; and how from thence she made her course to the tropical Latitude of the Great Pacific Ocean; and of the strange things that befell; and in what manner the Ancyent Marinere came back to his own Country.[18]

This, for anyone who has read Hakluyt or any other accounts of sea voyages bears an unmistakeable resemblance to their style. Coleridge was an avid reader of these nautical and travel journals as his notebooks show. He read ones written from the late sixteenth century up to those of his own time. One of his favourites was *Purchas his Pilgrimage* (1613). During the entire seventeenth century and into the nineteenth people were as much engrossed by exploration of the world as our own times are absorbed by journeys into space. Coleridge takes not only the style of the 'Argument' but also the settings and whole itinerary from an amalgam of voyages. These he worked out meticulously. More importantly for us he used a selection of the types of language, especially the vocabulary, found in these journals. Almost every word of any significance can be found somewhere or other in the journals. Under their influence Coleridge keeps the language matter-of-fact and avoids the supernatural language that he introduced early into *Christabel.* The vocabulary is mostly concrete, as indeed was that of *Christabel,* but it is arranged and combined in a way that is also concrete and factual, especially in Part I. The description of the ship's setting sail is typical:

> The Ship was cheer'd, the Harbour clear'd –
>   Merrily did we drop
> Below the Kirk, below the Hill
>   Below the light-house top.

The basic everyday, almost monosyllabic, vocabulary is very different from that of Coleridge's earlier poems. That scarcely a word or phrase in the topographical descriptions is Coleridge's own matters little. It is the way in which he pieces together and combines the words that is important and which allows him to set in motion the sequence of events.

In the course of three and a half stanzas, admittedly broken up by the reflections of the Wedding Guest, Coleridge brings the ship into the waters of the Antarctic. This indicates something of his economy of style in this poem. After a further six stanzas about the unnatural cold of these southern waters and the coming of the Albatross, the Wedding Guest directly addresses the Mariner for the first time since the opening stanza. The first climax is reached and the crucial deed stated:

> 'God save thee, ancyent Marinere!
>   'From the fiends that plague thee thus –
> 'Why look'st thou so?' –

and the Mariner replies:

>   With my cross-bow
> I shot the Albatross.

Thus is the salient fact that sets in train the rest of the strange and ghostly adventures expressed in a brief and simple clause. The words, apart from *albatross*, are all monosyllabic and there is no elaboration of any kind. The statement could not be more simple or more startling. The word order is, with a slight exception, that of the usual English clause structure – S V C. It could be said to be thematically marked by the initial prepositional phrase, which would more normally come at the end, but this contains the instrument of the action, the cross-bow. Instrument, actor and action make up one incident and by placing them together, Coleridge makes the Mariner's crime more telling. Had the prepositional phrase come after the complement, it would have lessened the force of the close-knit grouping Coleridge selected, In addition the *cross* is a recurrent theme and the thematic placing of the word here is significant. The one succeeding event that is as shocking in its unexpectedness, because it is expressed in a comparably naked way, is the ship's sinking at the end of its voyage. This is presaged by four lines of strange rumbling in the water but the climax is simply:

The Ship went down like lead.

This again uses monosyllables and, in spite of the simile, a commonplace one, is metrically briefer than the shooting of the Albatross.

Not only the concrete, if sometimes picturesque, descriptions of natural objects in the first part of the poem come from the sea journals. So also do the stranger details of natural phenomena and sea creatures in the part that follows the Mariner's crime. In Part I the Mariner tells of 'Ice mast-high' that was 'As green as Emerauld' and which 'crack'd and growl'd and roar'd and howl'd'. After the killing of the albatross we read that:

All in a hot and copper sky
  The bloody sun at noon,
Right up above the mast did stand,
  No bigger than the moon

and that:

The very deeps did rot: O Christ!
  That ever this should be!
Yea slimy things did crawl with legs
  Upon the slimy Sea.

This sinister-sounding account of the noon sun and the horrifying creatures that 'crawl with legs' on the sea are all documented, as are the Death-fires that dance on the waters at night while the sea:

            like witch's oils
Burnt green and blue and white.

Later, when the curse is partly lifted by the Mariner's blessing the 'water-snakes' in their rich colours of 'Blue, glossy green, and velvet black' – again authenticated details and words actually used – there is a mixture of the natural, if exotic, and the supernatural. There is also an alternation between the frightening and the strangely beautiful. Because of the strangeness of the natural objects, the supernatural is more readily accommodated and, indeed, credible, especially as Coleridge uses the same simple, everyday language to describe it.

It seems odd to find lyrically expressed descriptions of a countryside that is clearly English in a tale of the sea and an enchanted one at that, yet these too show the influence of the nautical journals.[19] The explorers, forced to describe strange sights in terms that could be understood, were accustomed to introduce familiar objects into their narratives and to use similes comparing the sights they met to the country scenery which their readers would know. Coleridge makes greatest use of this sort of simile in the ghostly parts of the tale but he has merely transferred it from the records of sea-life. Indeed, the land imagery enables him to construct a bridge between the factual and the spectral through the language. A striking example of this type of simile occurs when the inspirited corpses finish their tasks at dawn and begin to sing. It sounds to the Mariner as if:

> all little birds that are
> How they seem'd to fill the sea and air
> With their sweet jargonings.

Again, in this lyrical image only two words are not monosyllables, one being the very commonplace adjective *little* and the other the noun *jargonings*.[20] Meanwhile, the ship did not cease to pursue its homeward journey:

> yet still the sails made on
> A pleasant noise till noon,
> A noise like of a hidden brook
> In the leafy month of June,
> That to the sleeping woods all night
> Singeth a quiet tune.

In this case the simile is extended and conjures up the exact type of idyllic image of the English countryside found in the journals. A final lyrical touch is linked to the real-life land breeze that the Mariner feels as the ship nears the shore:

> It rais'd my hair, it fann'd my cheek,
>   Like a meadow-gale in spring.

The real and the supernatural come together in these lines as the Mariner hopes, yet fears to hope, that he has reached home:

> It mingled strangely with my fears,
>   Yet it felt like a welcoming.

The very word *welcoming*, especially in collocation with or contrast to *fears* has a homely sound.

For the horrors which the Mariner has to undergo Coleridge makes use of the same basic language and by so doing succeeds in creating an atmosphere as sinister as that created by the more expected type of language of *Christabel*. The dead sailors 'raise their arms like lifeless tools', an automaton-like touch that adds to the sense of unreality while still using everyday words. The following stanza continues:

> The body of my brother's son
>   Stood by me knee to knee:
> The body and I pull'd at one rope,
>   But he said nought to me.

The repetition of the word *body* together with its physical proximity, is also terrifying in its muteness.

Besides the sinister, or often in juxtaposition with it, Coleridge frequently suggests realism in a similarly vivid way. The eyes of the dead men are constantly alluded to:

> All fix'd on me their stony eyes
>   That in the moon did glitter.

Their eyes remain staring fixedly at the man who has brought about their death. Even when they are reanimated, they 'ne mov'd their eyes'. It is no wonder that the Mariner shuts his

Part five .

own to escape their gaze. But it is the exactness of the description of the still living eyes, as the Mariner tries to blot out the gruesome spectacle, that enables the reader to enter into his terror:

> I clos'd my lids and kept them close,
>   Till the balls like pulses beat.

The sensation of thirst slaked is also enhanced by comparison. The evocation of thirst is unforgettable in its detail:

> With throat unslack'd, with black lips bak'd
>   Ne could we laugh ne wail:
> Then while thro' drouth all dumb they stood
> I bit my arm and suck'd the blood
>   And cry'd, A sail! a sail!

The obverse of this horrible picture is:

> My lips were wet, my throat was cold,
>   My garments all were dank.

Without the vividness of the first description the sensation of the second would be less forceful. The most telling word in context is *cold* connected with *throat*, which makes the reader *feel* the quenching of the Mariner's thirst.

Coleridge uses basic vocabulary to build up the horror of the supernatural, as well as to suggest ordinary physical sensation, in such a way that the reader experiences the intensity of the Mariner's feelings. By contrast, Wordsworth uses similarly matter-of-fact diction and simple syntax to evoke the atmosphere of everyday life. Coleridge, by combining words and phrases into simple statements, with very few literary devices and even fewer departures from basic vocabulary, creates a world that could not be further removed from the everyday. His is the unexpected achievement. He conveys the supernatural through the natural. *The Ancyent Marinere* differs in this respect from *Christabel*; and possibly for this reason, at least in part, it was finished, whereas *Christabel* never was.

Coleridge wrote *The Ancyent Marinere* in the traditional ballad form. Earlier we considered Wordsworth's use of ballad language, especially in relation to 'Goody Blake and Harry Gill', but *The Ancyent Marinere* is a much longer poem and it is worth seeing how far Coleridge sustains the ballad style.

The metre consists mainly of alternating four and three foot iambic lines: v–v–v–v– / v–v–v–, in four-line stanzas. The rhyme scheme is, again basically, abcb. There are, however, very many variations in line and stanza length and in the rhyme pattern. Indeed, the very first stanza departs from the norm. There are also many internal rhymes, which occur in only a few traditional ballads.

Many traditional ballad features are incorporated in the poem, often with some slight variation. The most obvious example is the curse, which is central to many ballads. Instead of a spoken curse, however, Coleridge has a silent and infinitely more menacing one. The doomed sailors bring the curse on the Mariner as they drop lifeless on the deck of the ship:

> Each turn'd his face with a ghastly pang,
>   And curs'd me with his ee.

Nor does he leave it there, for it returns some time later:

> The look with which they look'd on me
>   Had never pass'd away.
>
> An orphan's curse would drag to Hell
>   A spirit from on high;
> But O! more horrible than that
>   Is the curse in a dead man's eye!
> Seven days, seven nights I saw that curse,
>   And yet I could not die.

Further on still, just before the spell of the curse is broken, there is another reminder:

> All stood together on the deck,
>   For a charnel-dungeon fitter:
> All fix'd on me their stony eyes,
>   That in the moon did glitter.

> The pang, the curse, with which they died,
>   Had never pass'd away.

Repetition, a feature of all Coleridge's poetic language, is prominent in *The Ancyent Marinere*, as it is in the ballads. There is repetition of every kind: words, phrases, whole clauses and syntactical structures. An extreme example of verbal repetition is:

> Alone, alone, all all alone,
>   Alone on the wide wide Sea.

Repetition of phrase and clause patterning combine in:

> The Ice was here, the Ice was there,
>   The Ice was all around.

There is at least one instance where the pattern is inverted:

> Down dropt the breeze, the Sails dropt down.

Occasionally a whole clause is repeated, usually with some slight variation at the end. At the turning point of the Mariner's misfortunes, when he is moved to bless the sea creatures, the clause 'And I bless'd them unaware' is repeated exactly. Doublets, another type of repetition typical of ballads, are found throughout: such phrases as 'well or sick'; and 'bliss or woe'; and the line:

> In mist or cloud on mast or shroud.

Coleridge does not make very much use of the formulaic phrases, which are typical of ballads and poetry based on an oral tradition, and which Wordsworth used. Occasionally one can be detected, as: 'nine fathom deep' in the line:

> Under the keel nine fathom deep,

and the entire line:

As sad as sad could be.

More often Coleridge fills a space where a formula might be expected with some more vivid and unexpected wording of his own:

> The lightning falls with never a jag,
>   A river steep and wide.

Here 'with never a jag' and the whole of the following line seem to be obvious places for stock phrases.
  Conversely, Coleridge uses many conventional similes: 'Red as a rose is she'; 'dry as dust'; and both the Albatross and the ship sink 'like lead'. There are, however, many much more striking and original similes. One, used in juxtaposition to one of the conventional type, comes in the description of Death's mate in the spectre ship:

> Her locks are yellow as gold:
>   Her skin is white as leprosy.

The conventional 'white as snow' might have been expected. Another vivid and apt comparison occurs when the souls of the dead sailors leave their bodies:

> And every soul, it pass'd me by,
>   Like the whizz of my Cross-bow!

This picks up the 'cross-bow' motif that occurs throughout the central part of the poem.
  Other figures of speech found to some extent in traditional-type ballads and which Coleridge uses are alliteration, as in 'the furrow followed free', although this is not very common in either the ballads or the poem, and stereotyped exclamations, such as 'Ah! well a day' and 'Gramercy!'. Description, apart from simile, is vivid, particularly when Coleridge depicts the wonders of the sea. Sufficient examples have already been quoted to illustrate this.
  Short co-ordinate clauses are typical of the syntax of *The Ancyent Marinere*, as of traditional ballads. Ballads frequently

change tense from the past to the present, especially at moments of climax. Such changes are found in *The Ancyent Marinere*. Just before the dead sailors stir into apparent life we read:

> The upper air burst into life,
> 　And a hundred fire-flags sheen
> To and fro they are hurried about;
> And to and fro, and in and out
> 　The stars dance on between.

Coleridge, however, changes tense frequently in a somewhat haphazard way and it is not always possible to deduce any particular reason. As in traditional ballads speeches are some-times presented in a dramatic way with no verb of saying:

> It is an ancyent Marinere,
> 　And he stoppeth one of three:
> 'By thy long grey beard and thy glittering eye,
> 　'Now wherefore stoppest me?'

In the 1800 edition of *Lyrical Ballads* many archaic words and spellings were dropped but some were retained, such as *anear*; *Iwist* and the spelling *countree* – probably sufficient to keep the feeling of a ballad. Oddly the word *eftsones* was omitted from line 527 but in 1817 was added, in the spelling *eftsoons*, to line 16. Certain grammatical and syntactical archaisms were also retained, one being the use of the empty auxiliary *do* in the past tense, as in 'The Ice did split'. Coleridge also uses a marked infinitive in certain places where it was no longer used in his time. This, too, is found in the ballads. One example is 'and it was He / That made the Ship to go'. He occasionally has a pleonastic pronoun, a feature which can be found in some ballads: 'O sleep, it is a gentle thing'. One feature that Coleridge does not use in any version is the omission of a relative pronoun in subject position, which is fairly common in some traditional ballads, as:

> And sent it to Sir Patrick Spence,
> 　Was walking on the sand.

The overall impression of Coleridge's final version is of a language that is timeless. Probably this has a more powerful effect on the imagination than the over-use of archaic language conveyed in the original.

The Ancyent Marinere sustains the traditional ballad style in a masterly fashion and is as good an example of pastiche as could be found. Yet Coleridge actually goes beyond the conventional. There is a sameness and a wooden quality in many genuine ballads that Coleridge avoids, both through his use of vivid language and simplicity of expression. An example of the extreme simplicity that he can attain occurs when the Mariner finally reaches his homeland and hardly dares to hope he is not dreaming. He says:

> We drifted o'er the Harbour bar,
>   And I with sobs did pray –
> 'O let me be awake, my God!
>   'Or let me sleep alway!'

The final two lines of this stanza sound almost like a hymn by Isaac Watts. One of Coleridge's most vivid descriptions is of the spirits who inhabit the bodies of the sailors:

> A man all light, a seraph-man,
>   On every corse there stood.
>
> This seraph-band, each wav'd his hand:
>   It was a heavenly sight!
> They stood as signals to the land,
>   Each one a lovely light.

This, in spite of including at least one stock phrase, is strangely beautiful as well as unearthly and it is no wonder that the Mariner says it strikes 'Like music on my heart'.

At the time of the writing of *Christabel* and *The Ancyent Marinere*, two years after he first met Wordsworth, Coleridge seems to have found his own peculiar poetic voice and language. That Wordsworth and Dorothy had something to do with it cannot be doubted but other less direct influences converged at this time. There are occasional felicities of expression in the early poems but they are sporadic and seem to be accidental. In the poems dealt with in this chapter Coleridge uses language with a conviction that was lacking until this period of 1797–8.

7   Analysis of Passages

Wordsworth's reputation during his lifetime reached its peak during the 1830s. It owed little to what we call *The Prelude*, which was published posthumously. Parts of this poem were, however, written as early as 1798 and a more or less full version, which was known to his friends, was complete by 1805. When Coleridge heard Wordsworth recite it in 1807 he was moved to praise it in blank verse. He included this eulogy in *Sybilline Leaves* in 1817 and referred to Wordsworth's poem in *Biographia Literaria* in the same year. Much that Coleridge said and believed about Wordsworth arose from his knowledge of this poem. He believed that Wordsworth was not only a great poet but should write the great philosophical poem that English still lacked. *The Prelude* (this title was never given to it by the poet himself) was for Wordsworth a prelude to this great philosophical work, proving to himself his fitness for the task. When at last it was published, it afforded the key to the rest of his life's work, and many later writers believe it was the crown of his poetic achievement. However that may be, Wordsworth himself thought highly enough of the poem to work over it for the rest of his life. Here, then, we shall examine two passages from *The Prelude*, using the 1805 text that Coleridge heard and admired in 1807.

The passages selected come from the skating scene in Book I and the reflective lines that follow. Throughout *The Prelude* Wordsworth describes particular incidents in his life and bases general philosophical and moral reflections on them. Often, as here, physical activities are recurrent:

And in the frosty season, when the sun   452
Was set, and visible for many a mile

The cottage windows through the twilight blaz'd,
I heeded not the summons: – happy time   455
It was, indeed, for all of us; to me
It was a time of rapture: clear and loud
The village clock toll'd six; I wheel'd about,
Proud and exulting, like an untired horse,
That cares not for its home. – All shod with steel,   460
We hiss'd along the polish'd ice, in games
Confederate, imitative of the chace
And woodland pleasures, the resounding horn,
The Pack loud bellowing, and the hunted hare.
So through the darkness and the cold we flew,   465
And not a voice was idle; with the din,
Meanwhile, the precipices rang aloud,
The leafless trees, and every icy crag
Tinkled like iron, while the distant hills
Into the tumult sent an alien sound   470
Of melancholy, not unnoticed, while the stars,
Eastward, were sparkling clear, and in the west
The orange sky of evening died away.

Wordsworth's development of a concrete and ordinary vocabulary in *Lyrical Ballads* had an undoubted effect on his later
writing, especially narrative poetry. The vocabulary here, with
a few exceptions, is matter-of-fact, much is monosyllabic, and
it presents a clear picture of the skating in the winter twilight.
The Latin origin of the two words *confederate* and *imitative* is an
exception, but in the context of the whole poem such literary
words do not seem out of place, even when, as here, there is an
inversion of noun and adjective: 'games / Confederate'. These
touches of more high-flown language in the descriptive or
narrative passages, together with corresponding concrete vocabulary in the reflective parts, assist the transition from one to
the other and make the necessary change of style less abrupt
and more acceptable. There are other abstract words, such as
summons and *rapture*, but these are less obtrusive.

Some of the usages differ slightly from those in *Lyrical
Ballads*. There are more premodifiers to nouns. In fact scarcely
a noun does not have at least one premodifier. There are also
far more adverbs, as distinct from adverbial clauses or phrases,

than in the earlier poems, although Wordsworth avoids adverbs ending in -*ly* and consequently it is not always possible to say if he intends an adverb or adjective. The village clock tolls 'clear and loud'; the boy moves 'proud and exulting' (an instance of ambiguity – do the words refer back to the verb *wheel'd* or the pronoun *I*?); the hounds bellow 'loud'; and the stars are sparkling 'clear'.

Verbs, too, are more striking and are frequently dynamic. The passage starts with a number of occurrences of the stative verb *to be*, but from the beginning more forceful verbs are used. The cottage windows, or the lights in them, 'blaze' (the inversion here is altered in the 1850 version to 'The cottage windows blazed through twilight gloom'); the clock 'tolls'; the boy 'wheels'; his companions 'hiss' on the ice, and later they 'flew'; the precipices 'rang'; and the trees and crags 'tinkled'. Many of these verbs are used metaphorically. The verb *sent*, when the hills send their 'alien' echo into the noise, is less forceful but typical of Wordsworth's use of an inanimate object, especially an object that is part of the natural scene, as the actor in a process more usually associated with human beings. More will be said about this in a moment. The final two verbs or verbal groups also seem to be less forceful. *Sparkling* is almost certainly a participle in a continuous tense rather than an adjective following *were*. Wordsworth rarely uses continuous tenses in his verse. He does occasionally when he is describing some natural process, although usually one spread over a period of time, such as the changing colours of leaves in autumn. The use here is especially vivid, partly because its time dimension is restricted. Finally, *dies away*, although a dynamic verb, carries an almost passive meaning: the action is one of withdrawal; but the sense of a diminuendo produces the right semantic cadence.

There has been much discussion of Wordsworth's intentions in the alterations which appeared in the first printed version of 1850. These need not detain us here.[1] In this passage, apart from restoring the inversion just mentioned to its more normal order, with the introduction of an additional word, *gloom*, there are only two changes in vocabulary, both substituting lexically empty words with more meaningful ones. The dynamic verb *smitten*, albeit in the passive participle form replaces *Meanwhile* in line 16. This is a verb of strong action. Two lines later 'the distant hills' is altered to *'far* distant hills', which further emphasises the vast scale of the landscape that surrounds the boys at play and adds to the effect of mystery introduced at this point.

The sentence structure of these lines is a mixture of Wordsworth's usual style of lengthy clause complexes and a fair number of shorter clauses. Generally, unlike the type of sentence in the blank verse poems of *Lyrical Ballads*, the main sentence elements, S V C, are not separated from each other. From line 455 the effect is of short statements, even when there is a lengthier clause, as in the long postmodification to *games* (lines 462–4). The most obviously lengthened sentence comes at the end of the extract, beginning at line 469 – 'while the distant hills'. It is at this point that the direct activity of the passage gives way to a more reflective mood. Even here there is simply a succession of three fairly short clauses.

In the midst of this unusually active scene, there are two examples of Wordsworth's typical negatively expressed statements carrying a positive meaning. The first: 'not a voice was idle', and the second, even more typical since it contains two negatives and omits any indication of a possible actor, such as is present in the word *voice*, the 'alien sound' is 'not unnoticed'.

The most interesting point is the amount of figurative language. Almost the whole is expressed through overt as well as grammatical metaphor and simile. The figurative expression can easily be overlooked, so down to earth does the description seem. For instance:

> All shod with steel
> We hiss'd along the polish'd ice

is clearly onomatopoeic, but in registering this aspect of the expression the reader very easily misses the metaphors 'shod with steel' – *steel* is also an example of metonymy (word association) – 'we hiss'd and 'the polish'd ice'. True, *shod* could be intended literally but coming immediately after the simile of the horse and in collocation with *steel* it seems that a metaphorical interpretation, with the idea expressed in the simile being carried forward, is more likely to be right.

Something should be said of the occasional destructive side of man in the natural world, which often strikes a discordant note in Wordsworth's accounts of childhood. This always occurs as part of man's learning process. In this passage it appears in the games the boys play: 'the woodland pleasures' which involve hunting innocent creatures. It is an aspect of youth that was apparent in a passage a little earlier when the poet describes his trapping of birds, 'all with springes hung. . . . a fell destroyer'. It also occurs in 'Nutting' in *Lyrical Ballads* when, after drinking in the atmosphere of the copse, the boy desecrates it for the sake of plundering the nuts. There is always some hint that these careless actions of youth are at odds with Nature, which seeks to tame the destructive forces. In this passage the process is less obvious than in the bird catching episode, in which the poet explicitly states:

> I was alone,
> And seem'd to be a trouble to the peace
> That was among them.

Here, the disparity between the boys and their carefree but cruel games and the spirit of the world of Nature is introduced more subtly and less through direct statement than by the implication of the expression. The two words *alien* and *melancholy* are set against the homely, joyful activity and they are both introduced in expanded nominal groups. *Alien* is a premodifier of *sound*, and the prepositional phrase, *of melancholy*, is its postmodifier. As elsewhere, the protracted effect of the loosely-knit group and the separation of *melancholy* from the head of the group *sound* by an intervening preposition forces the reader's attention onto the unexpected word *melancholy*. This is immediately followed by the double negative, *not unnoticed*, which has no stated actor. This may be unconsciously deliberate. The reader recognises the *alien sound* in a part-conscious way through the syntax, as the boy probably was half-consciously aware of it at the time. We saw in Chapter 5 how the syntax mirrored the apprehension of the young boy in much the same way in 'Michael'. The expanded construction here works in a similar way. The already long sentence is further lengthened by two additional adverbial clauses. The second of these contains another expanded construction, similarly using an *of* prepositional phrase: 'The orange sky of evening'. Although the preposition does not this time occur at the beginning of the line, as the prepositions of such expanded constructions frequently do, the clause itself runs over the line:

> in the west
> The orange sky of evening died away.

This has a similar effect of carrying a surge of energy over into the following line and the energy is diffused through the *of* phrase and the concluding verb. The verb and its extension *away*, which ends with an open syllable as well as a diphthong, itself has a lingering effect which draws out the sound in a way that matches the fading of light from the darkening sky.

This sense of the mysterious presence of presiding Nature comes again at the end of the second verse paragraph of this scene, when the boy, isolated from his companions, is more consciously aware – at least the awareness is more explicitly stated – of the surrounding hills, representing the forces of Nature. As they wheel by him, they appear to take on a life of their own.

This leads on to the second passage chosen for analysis, the meditative conclusion to this whole scene:

> Ye Presences of Nature, in the sky 490
> Or on the earth! Ye Visions of the hills!
> And Souls of lonely places! can I think
> A vulgar hope was yours when Ye employ'd
> Such ministry, when Ye through many a year
> Haunting me thus among my boyish sports, 495
> On caves and trees, upon the woods and hills,
> Impress'd upon all forms the characters
> Of danger or desire, and thus did make
> The surface of the universal earth
> With triumph, and delight, and hope, and fear, 500
> Work like a sea?

This, apart from the three apostrophising phrases at the beginning, is one sentence framed as a question, beginning 'can I think'. By the end it has become so much a statement that the final question mark is rather strange. Because of the length of this sentence, it should not surprise us that the structure is more complex than those in the first passage and therefore that the sense is less easy to follow. It is much more like those of the early blank verse poems. Wordsworth uses the device of resumption, which we have seen before. He repeats the *when* clause of line 493 in line 495. The second time he also separates the subject from the verb, first by a participial clause, and then by a succession of prepositional phrases, so that it is over two lines further on that we come to the verb *Impress'd*. This, in turn, is separated from its complement by a prepositional phrase, *upon all forms*. The final clause of the clause complex is a resultant clause, beginning 'and thus'. It is dependent on the two *when* clauses and again the subject, *The surface of the universal earth* is separated from its verb, *work*, by a series of prepositional phrases (in this case consisting of one-word complements), although only in the first phrase is the preposition *with* actually stated.

Predictably, the vocabulary of this extract is more abstract than that of the previous one but it is by no means wholly so. Nor, apart from the initial apostrophes, is it high-flown or literary, although the first impression is of an elevated and philosophising passage. Apart from the nominal group *boyish sports*, human activity is lacking, but the objects of the natural world are expressed quite as concretely as in the first extract: *caves*; *trees*; *woods*, and *hills* (twice) are all basic monosyllabic words. In contrast the first passage included *precipices*. In this respect, however, this passage is not entirely typical of the reflective passages. Most of them, while including a few concrete and basic words, contain more elevated words than are found here. This is one of the passages that include a relatively large number of words denoting emotions or related to emotions, and these account for most of the abstract vocabulary: *hope* (twice); *danger*; *desire*; *triumph*; *delight*, and *fear*. At least two of the words in the apparently expanded construction, 'The surface of the universal earth', which is the subject of the clause in which it occurs, are also abstract but the objects denoted are literal, if general.

Unlike the previous extract, this one contains comparatively

few verbs and these are not particularly striking, although *think*
is the only strictly non-dynamic one. Others are *employ'd*;
impress'd; *make*, and *work*. Some are more forceful than they at
first appear. *Impress'd* is a verb that Wordsworth frequently uses
and, even when used metaphorically, as it usually is, it is
sometimes intended almost literally. Here the metaphor is
clearer than usual because of its collocation with the word
character. The metaphor is of Nature as a printing press and, in
one sense, Wordsworth does mean that the emotions, the
'characters', are literally impressed on the 'surface of the universal earth'. (*Universal* is not tautologous, since Wordsworth means
earth in its sense of 'ground' rather than 'the globe'.)

The reality and common understanding of emotions at this
period has been discussed earlier. The combination of the first
emotions mentioned, apart from the alliteration, is significant:
danger and *desire* are closely related to the later *fear* and *delight*.
Fear, which gives an emotional thrill, is repeatedly mentioned by
Wordsworth as one of the sensations felt in his childhood and
clearly has a positive rather than a negative force. Furthermore,
in this context, verbs like *impress* and *employ* are weightier verbs
than are found in the earlier passage and intended to carry a
correspondingly weightier meaning. The 'Presences of Nature',
the 'Visions of the hills' and the 'Souls of lonely places', from
which, together with the use of the archaic pronoun *Ye*, the
passage derives its more elevated quality, require a fuller verb
than the simple near synonym *use*. 'Employ'd / such ministry' is
a statement that has the necessary impact and is, moreover,
important in Wordsworth's philosophy. The final verb *works*
seems to have less semantic weight but in the phrase 'Works
like a sea', in which the brief simile is almost drawn into the
verb, it is still semantically powerful. The restless movement of
the sea must be seen in opposition to the normally static surface
of the earth, earth and sea being here deliberately set side by
side, for its full significance to be apparent.

Wordsworth's use of doublets, such as 'danger or desire' in
line 498, has not been noted before and is very evident in these
passages. Doublets occur throughout Wordsworth's verse, especially the blank verse of *The Prelude*. However, Wordsworth
does not confine himself to doublets. Triple and quadruple
groups are just as frequent. The opening apostrophes are an

example of a triple construction, the first one of which incorporates a doublet: 'in the sky / Or on the earth'. Two instances of quadruple uses occur. The first at line 496 is broken into two sets of doublets: 'caves and trees' and 'woods and hills'. In the final example, at line 500, each noun is joined by a co-ordinating *and* to the previous one:

   With triumph, and delight, and hope, and fear.

Other examples will be found in the first passage examined and, indeed, it would not be easy to find an extract of any length that did not contain examples.

His experiments with language in 1798 enabled Wordsworth later to juxtapose lively narrative with meditative passages without any sense of incongruity or jarring. His ability to handle concrete and ordinary vocabulary allows one type of verse to merge into the other in a natural way. He can, although he does not always do so, express reflections and emotions with relatively simple words and without recourse to personification or any of the other figures of speech which he rejected as artificial and simply restricting poetic counters used in eighteenth-century poetry. The one personification that occurs time and time again in *The Prelude* is that of Nature but for Wordsworth this is, one feels, a natural rather than an artificial usage.

We have seen throughout these chapters that Wordsworth's vocabulary is drawn from the basic stock that would have been used by both educated and uneducated alike. This was quite different from much of the poetic diction of the previous century. In addition, Wordsworth used language in a way not previously considered poetic. The experiments in language in *Lyrical Ballads* undoubtedly influenced his later poetry, especially *The Prelude* and *The Excursion*, as well as the shorter poems and such important pieces as 'Resolution and Independence' and 'The Intimations Ode', which have not been discussed here. Although a more literary vocabulary is found in some of these poems, particularly the long poems in blank verse, there is always a core of words in common use and this was to affect all later poets. Again, Wordsworth made possible for later poets an almost boundless extension of subject matter as a result of the poems in *Lyrical Ballads*. No aspect or social sphere of human life could afterwards be considered too low for poetic expression. Helen Darbishire has said:

> He emancipated the poetic subject; and brought back poetic language to its source in the living tongue. Thanks to Wordsworth, Browning could take as subject Mr. Sludge the medium no less than Fra Lippo Lippi. Tennyson could develop a rustic theme with even a banal simplicity:
> 'Take your own time, Annie, take your own time.'
> And our twentieth-century poets can sweep, as we know, from Byzantine glories to damp housemaids on area steps, and can freely explore the possibilities of a poetic language which may range from the charged words of inscrutable nursery rhymes through every compelling idiosyncrasy of elliptical speech to the allusive lingo of learned scholarship.[2]

Wordsworth did not only extend the range of subject matter of poetry and the language that poets could use: he helped to shape the whole of the English imagination. His concentration on the effect of nature on man's thinking has conditioned people to look to the natural world as their true environment and spiritual home. In spite of continuing efforts to direct people towards urban life in poetry and in all other areas of culture and education, most Englishmen still dream of a 'cottage in the country'. Estate agents exploit this mercilessly. Every house that possibly can be is advertised as a 'cottage'. Holiday brochures tempt people to take a break from the monotony of work in towns at rural retreats with such fanciful names as Badger's Den, Heron's Nest, or the Hayloft, as well as every imaginable combination with 'cottage'. The power of this word *cottage*, or *cot(t)*, owes something to Coleridge, who uses the word, if anything, even more frequently than Wordsworth. The hankering after a life that looks 'back to nature' is peculiarly British.[3] Wordsworth's language cannot be separated from the subjects on which he chose to write. Nevertheless, he brought about a revolution in poetic expression and did it almost single-handed. It could be argued that he replaced one set of conventions governing poetic diction with another. However, his attitudes to language were far wider and all-embracing than those of the eighteenth-century poets. He was not only the first but also virtually alone in bringing everyday language deliberately into poetry of every kind.

8   Conclusion

> I was induced to request the assistance of a friend ... I
> should not, however, have requested this assistance, had I
> not believed that the Poems of my Friend would in a great
> measure have the same tendency as my own, and that,
> though there would be found a difference, there would be
> found no discordance in the colours of our style; as our
> opinions on the subject of poetry do almost entirely
> coincide.   (*LB*, p. 242)

Thus Wordsworth in the Preface of 1800 – the first edition of
Lyrical Ballads (1798) had been published anonymously. Although it was Coleridge who forced Wordsworth, somewhat
against his will, into writing the Preface, the attitude
Wordsworth adopts here suggests that he was the prime mover
in the publication. Perhaps it is for this reason, as much as any,
that Wordsworth has often been assumed to be the leader in
what was initially a joint enterprise. I said earlier that had he
not met Wordsworth we might now not hear of Coleridge the
poet. This does not mean, however, that Coleridge simply
followed where Wordsworth led. Undoubtedly Wordsworth
had a dedication to his craft and an ability to pursue a course
with a single-mindedness that Coleridge lacked. Wordsworth
wrote prolifically all his life and, although it is not examined
here, the later poetry is not all as mediocre as some critics have
thought. With such tenacity of purpose Wordsworth would
almost certainly have been a poet of stature without his
friendship with Coleridge; Coleridge might not have achieved
what he did without Wordsworth. What type of poetry
Wordsworth would have produced had he never met Coleridge
is, however, less clear. The early relationship between them

was, as already noted, too complex to be unravelled at this distance in time. But there are pointers and not all of them show Wordsworth as the dominant one of the pair.

That their 'opinions on the subject of poetry do almost entirely coincide' is true of the early years of their friendship and this applies both to language and subject matter. Both poets were in revolt against eighteenth-century diction and what they believed was a lack of depth and real sincerity of feeling in the poetry of the latter part of the century and the 'magazine' poetry of their own time. Both detected, as we have seen, a new depth in William Lisle Bowles. Just what they found new in Bowles may be difficult to appreciate today. Part of Bowles's sincerity is to be found in the language and move-ment of his verse. A brief glance back at the short extract quoted from one of his sonnets will show this (p. 8) There is a simplicity of expression here that both poets took into their own writing. There are indications, albeit slight, that Wordsworth was moving towards a more straightforward use of vocabulary in *Descriptive Sketches* (1791–2), which was written before he met Coleridge. Likewise, there are signs that Coleridge sporadically adopted a simpler diction in his early pieces, especially in the 'Eolian Harp' (1795). Indeed, the subject of this poem could be a synopsis of the so-called philosophy of Wordsworth's *Prelude*. In another early 'conversa-tion' poem of the same year, 'Reflections on Having Left a Place of Retirement', which is in the nature of a companion piece to 'The Eolian Harp', Coleridge again foreshadows both Wordsworth's 'message' and the type of language in which he expressed it in the line:

Blest hour! It was a luxury, – to be!

How much then did the one influence the other, or were their minds already moving in the same direction?

We know that the two discussed their ideas about poetry at length, but any notion that Wordsworth dominated these dis-cussions is unlikely. Coleridge was to gain a reputation as a voluble and brilliant virtuoso talker. He cannot have sat meekly by while Wordsworth pontificated. It is more likely that it was the other way about. Their ideas on suitable language for poetry: basic, simple diction and syntax, judicious use of rhetoric and figures of speech, including rejection of eighteenth-century personification, and all the other characteristics of their language that we have looked at must have grown out of these early discussions following the spring of 1797. They would have been fostered not only by similar opinions but also by the common reading matter of their early years. These discussions culminated in the following year in *Lyrical Ballads*.

Collaboration in a volume of verse came about almost accidentally. In order to finance the expenses of a walking tour they hit upon the idea of writing a poem together for the *Monthly Magazine*. This was to be *The Ancyent Marinere*. Soon after they started to write it, however, the differences between them, to which Wordsworth refers in the quotation above, became apparent, and Wordsworth, realising that it was more suited to the genius of his friend, withdrew from his share in its composition. They recognised that their common ideas on style and language could be better realised otherwise and so the plan of *Lyrical Ballads* was devised. Allowing for Coleridge's obvious talent for the supernatural:

> the thought suggested itself (to which of us I do not recollect) that a series of poems might be composed of two sorts. In the one, the incidents and agents were to be, in part at least, supernatural; and the excellence aimed at was to consist in the interesting of the affections by the dramatic truth of such emotions, as would naturally accompany such situations, supposing them real ... For the second class, subjects were to be chosen from ordinary life; the characters and incidents were to be such as will be found in every village and its vicinity, where there is a meditative and feeling mind to seek after them, or to notice them, when they present themselves. (*BL*, XIV, p. 168)

If this had been the complete plan, both poets might be said to have fulfilled their part of the deal. Whereas Coleridge was to write about 'persons and characters supernatural, or at least romantic' while at the same time they were to possess 'a semblance of truth sufficient to procure ... that willing suspension of disbelief for the moment, which constitutes poetic faith' (*BL*, XIV, pp. 168–9), Wordsworth was:

> to give the charm of novelty to things of everyday, and to excite a feeling analogous to the supernatural, by awakening the mind's attention to the lethargy of custom and directing it to the loveliness and the wonders of the world before us. (*BL*, XIV, p. 169)

Wordsworth's original counterpart to *The Ancyent Marinere* was *Peter Bell*, which seems indeed a fitting companion piece to Coleridge's poem and to perform the task set out in the quotation above. *Peter Bell* did not, however, appear in *Lyrical Ballads* and was not published until 1819. Instead Wordsworth contributed many of the poems we have examined, not all by any means in ballad form, as the title suggests.

The fact that they abandoned collaboration on *The Ancyent Marinere* and the evidence of the poems in *Lyrical Ballads* make it possible to say that just at the point when they were closest, Wordsworth and Coleridge began to draw apart. This is as true of the language as of any other aspect of their poetry and, indeed, it is probably accounted for as much by their different linguistic approach as by any difference in temperament. However, Wordsworth is right when he says 'there is no discordance in the colours of our style.' It is with essentially similar materials that they achieve such different results. However well Coleridge fulfilled his side of the bargain with *The Ancyent Marinere* (ironically it seems to have been this poem that impeded the initial success of the volume), it is the only poem of its type to appear in *Lyrical Ballads*. His other poems of the supernatural are all incomplete, and *The Ancyent Marinere* itself was written under the stern eye of Wordsworth, who even finished some parts when Coleridge's inspiration faltered. This does not mean that Coleridge's poems in other forms are less impressive, although, again, they are different from the types of poems Wordsworth wrote. Wordsworth also followed various different paths from those which they had laid down even in his first volume. The poetry of both writers is varied. Starting from a common stylistic theory they produced poetry that is surprisingly unlike. Few people would mistake the poetry of the one for that of the other.

Many similarities of language in the work of the two poets have been mentioned throughout this book, but important differences within the same basic framework have also emerged. Wordsworth's vocabulary, at least in the early poems, is more straightforward than that of Coleridge and is generally everyday and concrete. His use of abstract terms increased as he moved away from the early experiments in ballad metre but (with the possible exception of 'Goody Blake and Harry Gill') he never used diction to achieve the strange and sinister effects that Coleridge produces in *The Ancyent Marinere*. Coleridge was to use more exotic language in other poems of the supernatural and to revert to some extent to the Gothick vocabulary of the preceding years. In all his poetic forms that we have looked at, his vocabulary is richer and more colourful in its use of adjectives than that of Wordsworth. Wordsworth's diction, particularly when it moves into greater abstractness, has a less dense texture, which, combined with his predilection for circumlocutions and a looser sentence structure, gives his verse an aloofness and lofty grandeur that finds its natural outlet in the later blank verse. In syntax it is Coleridge who remains the more straightforward, whilst Wordsworth's sentence structure often becomes complex.

The figurative usages of the two poets are important since they are less straightforward than at first appears. Coleridge initially seems to use a wider range of figures of speech and to use them more frequently, but Wordsworth, in fact, relies more heavily on metaphor, perhaps, than any other English poet. Because this is not immediately obvious his meaning can sometimes appear simpler than it is. Coleridge's use of figurative language is more of the surface; Wordsworth's is built into the very matter of his poetry and the unwary reader can miss the full impact in consequence. Wordsworth may have abandoned the formal rhetoric of earlier poetry but he did not in the end discard figures of speech altogether. Instead they gradually worked themselves into the texture of his syntax and verse in such a way that they become part of his very means of thinking. He himself says in the 1802 Preface to *Lyrical Ballads*,

... if the Poet's subject be judiciously chosen, it will naturally, and upon fit occasion, lead him to passions the language of which, if selected truly and judiciously, must necessarily be dignified and variegated, and alive with metaphors and figures. (*LB*, pp. 254–5)

Although apparently less dependent on figurative language, therefore, Wordsworth's expression cannot be separated from his use of it and any attempt to do so empties the poetry of its meaning.

To try to evaluate which of the two poets had the greater influence on the other is a profitless task. Coleridge, although he continued to write verse until his death at the age of sixty-three, never devoted himself to it after the early 1800s with the same energy that Wordsworth gave to it over a life of eighty years. On the other hand, without Coleridge Wordsworth might have followed a different course. Coleridge, the philosopher, tried to make Wordsworth the philosopher-poet that he himself could not be. In the poems of *Lyrical Ballads*, however, when Wordsworth was finding his own voice, he shows much more interest in the states of mind of what might be called today the drop-outs' of society as well as ordinary humble folk, and also in social problems. Were he writing at the close of the twentieth century the climate of the time would almost certainly have pushed him towards the sociological. *The Prelude* might not have been written.

The course of English poetry probably owes as much to Coleridge as to Wordsworth, at least in style and language. Little that is in Wordsworth cannot be found in Coleridge and much of it can be identified first in Coleridge's early poetry. It is Wordsworth's new style of rhetoric and expression, however, that marks more clearly the starting point of modern poetry and made a return to the stylised forms of earlier times impossible. Moreover, his poetry, much as it owes to Coleridge, influences English popular thinking even today.

The names of Wordsworth and Coleridge remain inextricably linked through circumstance. Their poetry is ultimately different. In spite of that, Wordsworth's claim that they held similar opinions on language and style is true and the similarities appear in the poetry of both, which makes it surprising that agreement could produce such different results. The reason for this divergence will yield themselves only to a close investigation of the language they use. This study is a first and simplified step of such an investigation.

Notes

Where full bibliographical details of a book are not included in the notes they will be found in the Bibliography.

Chapter 1

1. In a letter from Mary Wordsworth to Sara Coleridge, written on 7 November 1845, recalling William and Dorothy's recollection of first seeing her father.

2. Mark L. Reed takes a somewhat different view in 'Wordsworth, Coleridge, and the "Plan" of the *Lyrical Ballads*' (1965), in *Coleridge: A Casebook*, eds Jones and Tydeman, pp. 117–35. This was written in answer to A. M. Buchan, 'The Influence of Wordsworth on Coleridge, 1795–1800' (1963) in the same volume, pp. 136–59.

3. The date 1704 refers to the first part of *Windsor-Forest*, which deals with nature. The second part, beginning at line 289, was composed in 1713, the year of publication.

4. William Taylor's translations had been circulated in MS. since the early 1790s. His version of 'Leonore' appeared in the *Monthly Magazine* in March, 1796. Scott had heard it read in Edinburgh in 1794 and it inspired his own translation.

5. No separate edition of *Songs of Experience* is known. It was attached to a new edition of *Songs of Innocence* in 1794.

6. '"When Bowles's sonnets first appeared," he said, "in a thin quarto pamphlet entitled *Fourteen Sonnets*, I bought them in a walk through London with my dear brother who was afterwards drowned at sea. I read them as we went along, and to the great annoyance of my brother, I stopped in a niche of London Bridge to finish the pamphlet."' Quoted from Mary Moorman, I, p. 125. In *Recollections of the Table Talk of Samuel Rogers*, ed. A. Dyce (London, 1856), p. 258, n. See also Reed, *CEY*, p. 95.

7. In the Preface to the 1805 edn. of his *Sonnets* Bowles says that they describe his personal feelings', occasioned by the death of the woman he loved.

8. See Grammatical Terminology, p. x.

9. STC says, 'If a writer, every time a compounded word suggests

itself to him, would seek for some other mode of expressing the same sense, the chances are always greatly in favour of his finding a better word.'

10. See Basil Willey, *The Eighteenth-Century Background*, p. 200. Willey is here citing J. S. Mill on the philosophy of the time but the same holds good for language.

11. M. A. K. Halliday and Ruqaiya Hasan, *Cohesion in English* (London: Longman, 1976), p. 71.

12. See *BL*, X (pp. 91–2). For a study of the language of Coleridge's prose see Timothy Corrigan, *Coleridge, Language, and Criticism.*

Chapter 2

1. Mary Jacobus, *Tradition and Experiment in Wordsworth's Lyrical Ballads, (1978)*. See particularly Ch. IX, pp. 209–32.

2. Verbs are divided into two principal categories: dynamic verbs ('action' verbs) such as *go*; *cry*; *feel* (in the physical sense); *tell* and stative verbs, which as their name implies refer to states, such as *be*; *seem*; *feel*; *know*; *think* and so on. Most copula verbs are also stative verbs and, because they do not denote actions, they are often called lexically empty, as are auxiliary verbs, such as *have* (when it is functioning as an auxiliary); *shall*; *will*. Verbs of 'inert perception' are stative verbs, requiring no volition on the part of the agent. Examples are verbs of the senses: *see*; *smell*; *hear*. Wordsworth writes 'The eye it cannot chuse but see' ('Expostulation and Reply'). However, in Wordsworth's poetry these distinctions, as so much else in his language, often become blurred. When he uses *see* of mental activity: 'We see into the life of things' ('Tintern Abbey') he seems to imply a deliberate act.

3. See Grammatical Terminology, p. x.

4. See Halliday, *IFG*, p. 62; and for an explanation of 'theme' pp. 38–40.

5. In the note to 'The Thorn' of 1800 Wordsworth maintained that the simple repetition of the same words did not necessarily constitute tautology: 'virtual tautology is much oftener produced by using different words when the meaning is exactly the same.' For him repetition of a word actually helped to create the feeling being conveyed; to the mind words are 'not only as symbols of the passion, but, as *things*, active and efficient, which are themselves part of the passion.' (*LB*, p. 289). This seems near to the eighteenth-century idea that to name the emotions was sufficient to recreate them for the reader (see p. 85). For Wordsworth, however, constant use of a certain word, and others related to it through the whole of his poetic output establishes a particular meaning for that word that exists in his poetry alone. In this way he creates his own language, or idiolect, in which he must be read. To a greater or lesser extent all poets create their own language but by

discussing it, Wordsworth showed a greater word-awareness than any other poet before him.

6. Reed, *CEY*, p. 32.

7. Mary Jacobus, p. 250: 'The opening stanza of 'The Idiot Boy' teasingly echoes the exclamatory refrains of Taylor's *Monthly Magazine* translation of Burger's 'Leonore' – "The moone is bryghte, and blue the nyghte" and "Halloo! Halloo! away they goe". Taylor's translation is reproduced in Jacobus, Appendix II, 277–83.

8. i.e. *girth*. *Girt* was in general usage in the seventeenth and eighteenth centuries but thereafter in the sense 'girth of a horse' was obsolete except in dialect. It seems possible that this is, therefore, already a dialectal usage.

9. In an introductory essay to *The Poetical Works of Robert Anderson* (1820) 'on the character, manners, and customs of the peasantry of Cumberland' Thomas Anderson wrote 'Most of ["the peasants of the present day"] can read, write, and cast up accounts', p. xliv. Both WW and Southey were subscribers to this volume. WW also wrote in a letter 'To the Editor of the Kendal Mercury', 12 April 1838: 'Further, it is well known that readers in the humbler ranks of society are multiplying most rapidly'. *PW*, III, 309.

10. Johnson's *Dictionary* (1755) shows the main stress falling as now on the first syllable, but the *OED* records that earlier it was pronounced with the stress on the second syllable. The 1838 edn. of Walker's *Rhyming Dictionary* (1828), still shows the stress on the second syllable. WW could therefore have pronounced the word either way.

11. Mary Jacobus disagrees with this interpretation in 'The Idiot Boy' in Jonathan Wordsworth, ed. *Bicentenary Wordsworth Studies*, pp. 238–65.

12. See *The Diary of Henry Crabb Robinson* in Cowell, ed. *Critics on Wordsworth*, p. 7. Part of the entry for 9 May 1815 says, 'But on my gently alluding to the lines: "Three feet long and two feet wide", and confessing that I dare not read them out in company, he said, "They ought to be liked"'.

13. See Hugh Sykes Davies, *Wordsworth's Worth of Words*. Unfortunately this study appeared too late to be used in this book but Chapter 9, on repetition and tautology in 'The Thorn', is worth reading in conjunction with this chapter.

Chapter 3

1. See Halliday *IFG*, pp. 187–90 for an explanation of the relation between phrase and clause.

2. See Halliday *IFG*, pp. 319–21 for metaphor and 'grammatical metaphor'. This is not an entirely new idea but is here explained for the first time in grammatical terms.

3. See Ward, *Wordsworth's Language of Men*, p. 187. Ward, in fact, argues that WW's language is metonymic rather than metaphoric, that

is the substitution of words is associative rather than symbolic. The distinction need not detain us here, although it partly accounts, perhaps, for the narrow line between what appears to be metaphor and what, in WW's philosophy, is perhaps intended as literal.

4. This example is taken from Halliday *IFG*, p. 322.

5. Halliday *IFG*, p. 321. Helen Darbishire made a similar comment in 1950, although not expressed in such overtly linguistic terms: 'This way of using images belongs to all language: our own speech is full of dormant, or dead, or half-alive metaphors.' *The Poet Wordsworth*, p. 165.

6. William Hazlitt, 'Mr Wordsworth', in *The Spirit of the Age: or Contemporary Portraits* (1825), P. P. Howe, ed. *The Complete Works of William Hazlitt*, vol. XI (London: Dent, 1932), pp. 86–95. Also quoted in Cowell, *Critics on Wordsworth*, p. 12.

7. Helen Darbishire, p. 164. The examples she gives are all connected with the use of emotion flowing through some aspect of human experience. Two from the poems here are:

To her fair works did Nature link
The human soul that through me ran,

from 'Lines Written in Early Spring', and:

Our souls shall drink at every pore
The Spirit of the Season,

from 'Lines written at a small distance from my house'. 'Drink at every pore' she links to the same notion of a spiritual or mental process being expressed as a physical one.

8. Hugh Sykes Davies points out that Wordsworth uses *impulse* consistently in a sense analogous to that of seventeenth-century philosophers. He writes, 'For [Wordsworth], it meant not an inexplicable eddy *within* the human spirit, but a movement stirred in it from *without* an influence upon the individual of some force in the outer universe' 'Wordsworth and the Empirical Philosophers', *The English Mind*, eds Hugh Sykes Davies and G. Watson (Cambridge: CUP, 1964), p. 155.

9. For further clarification of this point see Halliday *IFG*, p. 327.

10. See Reed, *CEY*, p. 32 for all the poems mentioned here.

Chapter 4

1. The dating of 'The Ruined Cottage' is complex. The story of Margaret was probably begun in March 1797 and was certainly in a fairly advanced state by June of that year. Most of the remaining part was probably written early in 1798 and finished by early March. It could have been written between June and July 1797 but this seems unlikely. See Reed, *CEY*, pp. 27–8, 337–9; see also *The Ruined Cottage*

and The Pedlar, ed. James Butler, Preface, x–xi and, for more detail, 'Introduction' pp. 3–35.

2. The final clause of the first line of the quotation was not completed until sometime between February and November 1799. See Butler, p. xi and pp. 48–9. The transcript of MS. D., in which it first appears, is on p. 289.

3. A plosive consonant is in one which the airstream is blocked by the tongue, teeth or lips and released suddenly. Examples in this line are *b; d; g; c.*

4. That the lines were in place by June 1797 is apparent from a letter of STC to John Estlin, written on 10 June 1797, to which they were attached. *Letters*, I, 327–8. See also Butler, p. 95 for transcript.

5. The lines about the spider's web were probably not omitted until MS. E, written 21 November 1803 to 18 March 1804. See Butler, p. xi and p. 416.

6. These lines appear only in the first draft (MS. A) of spring 1797 and there, after several attempts, are finally crossed out. See Butler, pp. 80–1. For the remarks on the Pedlar see Butler, pp. 85–7.

7. See also Butler, p. 17.

8. *Pebble, stone*, etc., are not really specific words within the compass of the generic word *rock*, because they refer to size only. Rocks can, of course, be classified in mineral or geological terms but this is outside the scope of the type of vocabulary we are considering here. Frequently, these sorts of words are mass rather than count nouns.

9. See Grammatical Terminology, p. xi.

10. See Chapter 5 on expanded syntax, pp. 100–3

11. 'The Brothers' was begun by 24 December 1797 and completed probably in early 1800. See Reed, *CEY*, p. 36. 'Michael', as it appears in *LB*, was written between 11 October and 9 December 1800. See Reed, *CMY*, p. 20.

12. Josephine Miles, *Wordsworth and the Vocabulary of Emotion*, p. 43. This is a useful book for understanding the background of the vocabulary of emotion in the eighteenth century, as well as its influence on WW and STC.

13. Ibid., p. 15.

14. See Frank B. Snyder, 'Wordsworth's Favourite Words', *Journal of English and Germanic Philology*, xxii (1923), 253–6.

15. All the following examples are from 'Tintern Abbey' unless otherwise stated.

16. See Chapter 2 n. 2 for an explanation of the term 'stative' verbs.

17. WW comments on the verb *hang* in its literal and metaphorical senses in *PW*, III, 31 (Preface of 1815). This is partially quoted in Chapter 3, p. 59.

Chapter 5

1. A sentence as understood here is the grammatical unit, not the punctuated unit.

2. There are exceptions, particularly in the reflective passages. In addition it is not always easy to be absolutely certain if clauses following a noun are restrictive and therefore part of the nominal group, or elaborating (non-restrictive) and therefore *not* part of it. WW very often uses a restrictive relative clause and gradually, as the original object of definition is left further behind, the syntax loosens until subsequent clauses are essentially non-restrictive and elaborating.

3. This effect has also been noticed by Howard S. Babb in *Jane Austen's Novels: the Fabric of Dialogue* (Hamden, Conn.: Archon Books, 1967), pp. 10–11.

4. For a fuller treatment of this subject see Frances Austin, 'Time, Experience and Syntax in Wordsworth's Poetry' in *Neuphilologische Mitteilungen*, LXX (1969), 724–37. Much of the substance of this article is reproduced here and in Chapter 7.

5. WW is attempting to express his sense of the inexpressible – 'something far more deeply interfused'. This 'something' can be *apprehended* from the 'setting sun', etc., in which the 'something', therefore, dwells, but it cannot be understood.

6. *Motion* is a word that can only take a causative transitive verb, such as *makes* – 'the motion of the car makes (causes me to be) sick'. WW follows it with an intransitive verb.

7. For an examination of WW's use of transitive verbs in 'Nutting' and the interplay between transitive and intransitive see Murray, *Wordsworth's Style*, pp. 63–8.

8. According to Reed, *CEY*, p. 333, a poem akin to the story of 'The Female Vagrant' may have been written by 1791 although no record of this exists. 'Salisbury Plain', later lengthened into the more ambitious 'Adventures on Salisbury Plain' was composed between 1795 and 1799. In spite of various attempts, it was not published and the story of the woman was extracted and recast in a different verse form to appear in *LB* of 1798. WW revised the original MS. in 1841 and it was published as 'Guilt and Sorrow' in 1842. See *The Salisbury Plain Poems*, ed. Stephen Gill (Ithaca, New York: Cornell U.P. & Hassocks, Sussex: Harvester Press, 1975), pp. 3–4.

9. The character of the Pedlar was originally introduced simply as the narrator of the story of Margaret when the poem was begun in 1797. The 'Ruined Cottage' of 1798 included first a brief history of the Pedlar and subsequently a lengthy account of the development of his mind. In 1799 WW separated the story of the Pedlar from the rest of the poem and it appears in an Addendum in MS. D. In 1802 he returned to the Addendum and composed a poem entitled 'The Pedlar', which contained the story of the Pedlar only but in 1803–4 he recombined the two parts of the poem, which were thereafter known as 'The Pedlar'. See Butler, Preface x–xii.

10. Milton, in fact, is not as Latinate as previously thought, although he does use some Latinate constructions, including this. See Thomas N. Corns, *The Development of Milton's Prose Style* (Oxford: Clarendon Press, 1982).

11. The 'Description of a Beggar', which was purely descriptive, was the earliest version of both 'The Old Man Travelling', which appeared in *LB* of 1798 and 'The Old Cumberland Beggar', which was published in *LB* of 1800. It was probably composed between the second half of 1796 and early June 1797. The first version of 'The Old Cumberland Beggar', which WW described as 'an overflowing' from 'The Old Man Travelling', probably existed as an independent poem in early 1798. The published version was composed later, probably between the end of April 1799 and 10 October 1800. See Reed, *CEY*, pp. 27, 342–3.

12. WW makes several apparently abortive attempts to start the narrative before this but each time he returns to description of one kind or another.

Chapter 6

1. One of the most recent appraisals of Jakobson's work in this area is 'The Poetic Function and the Nature of Language' by Linda R. Waugh in Roman Jakobson: *Verbal Art, Verbal Sign, Verbal Time*, eds Krystyna Pomorska and Stephen Rudy (Oxford: Blackwell, 1985), pp. 155–7.

2. For a synopsis of Hartley's ideas see R. C. & Kathleen Oldfield, 'Hartley's Observations on Man', *Annals of Science*, 7 (1951), 371–81. See also Basil Willey, *The Eighteenth-Century Background*, Ch. 8, pp. 133–49.

3. STC, *The Critical Review*, August 1794, p. 361.

4. Vowels are described in terms of tongue position. A closed vowel is one in which the jaws are held close together and the tongue is near the roof of the mouth, allowing only a narrow aperture for the airstream to pass through. In an open vowel the bottom jaw and the tongue are lowered. Various mid-points occur. /i:/ as in *meet* is the highest front vowel; /ɑ:/ – the sound the doctor asks a patient to say in order to examine his throat – is the lowest back vowel.

5. See Ward, *Wordsworth's Language of Men*, pp. 39–54.

6. Ibid., p. 43.

7. Ibid., p. 45.

8. Ibid., p. 51.

9. George Sampson, *The Concise Cambridge History of English Literature* (Cambridge: CUP, 1944), p. 581.

10. The Aeolian harp is called after Aeolus, the Greek god of winds. The instrument was revived in Germany in the early seventeenth century and STC actually possessed one.

11. Lines 30–3 were added in 1803; lines 26–9 in 1817.

12. There are instances in WW's poems of undefined individuals, as

in 'The Old Cumberland Beggar' but this is done for a particular purpose and is not the equivalent of STC's example here.

13. The superstitious belief that the flameless film that flickers over a fire denotes the arrival of a stranger is widespread.

14. Henry Nelson Coleridge in *Quarterly Review*, LII (August 1834), 29. This extract is reprinted in Jones and Tydeman, pp. 83–5.

15. William Hazlitt in the *Examiner* (2 June 1816) recalls that the original MS. ran 'thus, or nearly thus:

Behold her bosom and half her side –
Hideous, deformed, and pale of hue.'

He believes this is the 'keystone' of the whole poem and considers it a 'psychological curiosity' that Coleridge later substituted the line now known. An extract from this piece by Hazlitt is reprinted in Jones and Tydeman, pp. 62–5. The full text is in *The Complete Works of William Hazlitt*, ed. P. P. Howe (London: Dent, 1930–4), XIX, 32–4.

16. STC's Preface to the 1816 edition of 'Christabel' can be found in *Poetical Works*, ed. E. H. Coleridge, I, 213–5.

17. See John Livingstone Lowes, *The Road to Xanadu, passim.*

18. The 'Argument' was changed considerably in the edition of 1800 and thereafter omitted.

19. Livingstone Lowes, pp. 195–7.

20. *Jargonings* should not be confused with the present-day word *jargon*. It is a revival of a medieval word and Coleridge probably took it from Chaucer's *The Romaunt of the Rose*. See Livingstone Lowes, pp. 333–4 for evidence to support this theory.

Chapter 7

1. See for changes in the various versions Mary Burton, *The One Wordsworth*, and Mary Burton, 'How Wordsworth Changed the Diction of *The Prelude*', *College English*, iii, 1941, 12–24.

2. Helen Darbishire, *The Poet Wordsworth*, pp. 56–7.

3. For a discussion of Wordsworth's own attitude to nature and urbanisation see Hugh Sykes Davies, *Wordsworth and the Worth of Words*, Part IV, esp. pp. 238–48.

Select Bibliography and Further Reading

Texts and Reference

COLERIDGE, S. T., *Collected Letters of Samuel Taylor Coleridge*, 6 vols. ed. Earl Leslie Griggs (Oxford: Clarendon Press, 1956–71).

COLERIDGE, S. T., *The Poetical Works of Samuel Taylor Coleridge*, 2 vols. ed. Ernest Hartley Coleridge (Oxford: Clarendon Press, 1975, 1st pub. 1912).

COWELL, RAYMOND (ed.), *Critics on Wordsworth* (London: George Allen & Unwin, 1973).

JONES, ALUN R. and TYDEMAN, WILLIAM (eds), *Coleridge: The Ancient Mariner and other Poems; A Casebook* (London: Macmillan, 1973).

JONES, ALUN R. and TYDEMAN, WILLIAM (eds), *Wordsworth: Lyrical Ballads; A Casebook* (London: Macmillan, 1972).

LOGAN, JAMES V., *Wordsworthian Criticism* (New York: Gordian Press, 1961, repr. 1974).

REED, MARK L., *Wordsworth: The Chronology of the Early Years 1770–1799* (Cambridge, Mass.: Harvard University Press, 1967).

REED, MARK L., *Wordsworth: The Chronology of the Middle Years 1800–1815* (Cambridge, Mass.: Harvard University Press, 1975).

WORDSWORTH, DOROTHY, *The Journals of Dorothy Wordsworth*, 2 vols. ed. Ernest de Selincourt (London: Macmillan, 1941).

WORDSWORTH, WILLIAM, *Poetical Works*, 5 vols. ed. Ernest de Selincourt and Helen Darbishire (Oxford: Clarendon Press, 1940–9).

WORDSWORTH, WILLIAM, *The Prelude*, ed. Ernest de Selincourt (Oxford: Clarendon Press, 1926, rev. Helen Darbishire, 1959).

WORDSWORTH, WILLIAM, *The Prose Works of William Wordsworth*, 3 vols. eds W. J. B. Owen and Jane Worthington Smyser (Oxford: Clarendon Press, 1974).

WORDSWORTH, WILLIAM, *Wordsworth's Literary Criticism*, ed. W. J. B. Owen (London: Routledge & Kegan Paul, 1974).

WORDSWORTH, WILLIAM and DOROTHY, *The Letters of William and Dorothy Wordsworth*, 6 vols. ed. Ernest de Selincourt (Oxford: Clarendon Press, 1935–8).

WORDSWORTH, WILLIAM and DOROTHY, *The Letters of William and Dorothy Wordsworth*, 2nd edn., 7 vols. (Oxford: Clarendon Press, 1967–88).

I. *The Early Years 1787–1805*, ed. and rev. Chester L. Shaver, 1967.
II. *The Middle Years 1806–1811*, ed. and rev. Mary Moorman, 1969.
The Middle Years 1812–1820, ed. and rev. Mary Moorman and Alan G. Hill, 1970.
III. *The Later Years 1821–1828*, ed. and rev. Alan G. Hill, 1978.
The Later Years 1829–1834, ed. and rev. Alan G. Hill, 1980.
The Later Years 1835–1839, ed. and rev. Alan G. Hill, 1982.
The Later Years 1840–1853, ed. and rev. Alan G. Hill, 1988.
WORDSWORTH, WILLIAM and COLERIDGE, S. T., *Lyrical Ballads*, eds R. L. Brett and A. R. Jones (London: Methuen, 1963, rev. 1965).

Background

GRANT, ALLAN, *A Preface to Coleridge* (London: Longman, 1972).

GROOM, BERNARD, *The Unity of Wordsworth's Poetry* (London: Macmillan, 1966).

MOORMAN, MARY, *William Wordsworth: A Biography*, 2 vols. (Oxford: Clarendon Press, 1957 and 1965).

PURKIS, JOHN, *A Preface to Wordsworth* (London: Longman, 1970).

WILLEY, BASIL, *Samuel Taylor Coleridge* (London: Chatto & Windus, 1972).

WILLEY, BASIL, *The Eighteenth-Century Background* (London: Chatto & Windus, 1940; Penguin Books, 1962).

Studies

AUSTIN, TIMOTHY R., 'Stylistic Evolution in Wordsworth's Poetry: Evidence from Emendations', *Language and Style*, 12 (1979) 176–87.

BURGUM, EDWIN B., 'Wordsworth's Reform in Poetic Diction', *College English*, 2 (1940) 207–16.

BURTON, MARY E., 'How Wordsworth Changed the Diction of *The Prelude*', *College English*, 3 (1941) 12–24.

BURTON, MARY E., *The One Wordsworth* 2nd edn. (Hamden, Conn.: Archon Books, 1972, 1st pub. 1942).

CORRIGAN, TIMOTHY, *Coleridge, Language and Criticism* (Athens, Ga: Georgia University Press, 1982).

DARBISHIRE, H., *The Poet Wordsworth* (Oxford: Clarendon Press, 1950).

DAVIES, HUGH SYKES, *Wordsworth and the Worth of Words*, eds John Kerrigan and Jonathan Wordsworth (Cambridge: Cambridge University Press, 1986).

FERGUSON, FRANCES, *Wordsworth: Language as Counter-Spirit* (New Haven: Yale University Press, 1977).

HARTMAN, GEOFFREY H., *Wordsworth's Poetry 1787–1814* (New Haven: Yale University Press, 1964).

HINCHLIFFE, KEITH, 'Wordsworth and the Kinds of Metaphor', *Studies in Romanticism*, 23 (1984) 81–100.

HOUSE, HUMPHREY, *Coleridge* (London: Rupert Hart-Davis, 1953).

JACOBUS, MARY, *Tradition and Experiment in Wordsworth's* Lyrical Ballads (1798) (Oxford: Clarendon Press, 1976).

LOWES, JOHN LIVINGSTONE, *The Road to Xanadu* (London: Constable, 1927).

MARKS, EMERSON R., *Coleridge on the Language of Verse* (New Jersey: Princeton University Press, 1981).

MILES, JOSEPHINE, *Wordsworth and the Vocabulary of Emotion*, 2nd ed. (New York: Octagon Books, 1965; 1st pub. University of California Press, 1942).

MURRAY, ROGER N., *Wordsworth's Style: Figures and Themes in the Lyrical Ballads of 1800* (Lincoln: University of Nebraska Press, 1967).

WARD, J. P., *Wordsworth's Language of Men* (Brighton, Sussex: Harvester Press, 1984).

WORDSWORTH, JONATHAN, (ed.), *Bicentenary Wordsworth Studies* (Ithaca, New York: Cornell University Press, 1970).

Index 1   Textual References

Note   Numbers at the end of a series, written thus: 2.4, refer to the Notes. 2.4 would indicate: Notes, Chapter 2, note 4.

Wordsworth: Poems

Adventures on Salisbury Plain, 5.8
Anecdote for Fathers, 47, 48, 49, 51, 52–3, 60
Borderers, The, 3, 93, 117
Brothers, The, 64, 68, 78–81, 84, 86, 97–8, 101, 114, 115–17, 118–19, 120–1, 4.11
Brougham Castle, Song at the Feast of, 151
Description of a Beggar, 5.11
Descriptive Sketches, 12, 13, 104–5, 106, 181
Discharged Soldier, The, 93, 105, 111, 112
Evening Walk, An, 12, 103–4, 105
Excursion, The, 65, 110, 177
Expostulation and Reply, 47, 58, 60, 103
Female Vagrant, The, 12, 13, 15, 21, 28, 81, 110, 141, 5.8
Fountain, The, 48, 51–4, 60–1
Goody Blake and Harry Gill, 16, 18, 20–1, 22–3, 24–5, 163, 183
Guilt and Sorrow, 13, 5.8
Hart-Leap Well, 148, 151
Idiot Boy, The, 21, 22, 24, 25–36, 37, 48, 60, 68
If Nature for a Favorite Child, 50–1
Immortality, Intimations of, 69, 79, 177
Last of the Flock, The, 17–18, 19–20, 23, 24, 36–40, 44, 56–7, 60, 87
Lines written in early spring, 57
Lucy poems, 47, 49, 61, 63, 90
   She dwelt among th'untrodden ways, 49, 50, 61–3, 90

slumber did my spirit seal, A, 61, 62–3
Strange fits of passion have I known, 61
Lyrical Ballads, 2, 3, 13, 57, 93, 170–1, 172, 177–8, 182, 183, 185
Mad Mother, The, 20, 24
Matthew poems, 47, 60–1, 121
   The Fountain, 48, 51–4, 60–1
   If Nature for a favorite Child, 50–1
   The Two April Mornings, 60–1
Michael, 64, 67, 81–4, 87, 94–5, 97, 101, 102–3, 105–6, 108–9, 115, 117–21, 173
Naming of Places, Poems on, 76
Nutting, 173, 5.7
Old Cumberland Beggar, The, 64, 68, 76–8, 89, 91, 95–7, 100–1, 109–10, 115, 5.11
Old Man Travelling, The, 5.11
Pedlar, The, 5.9
Peter Bell, 183
Prelude, The, 3, 73–6, 85–6, 87–8, 92, 93, 100, 101, 102, 111, 114, 126, 131, 169–79, 181, 185
Resolution and Independence, 7, 59, 177
Ruined Cottage, The, 13, 65–7, 68–9, 72, 80, 93, 101, 105, 110, 111, 112, 139, 4.1, 4.5, 4.6, 5.9
Ruth, 81
Salisbury Plain, 13, 110, 5.8
She dwelt among th'untrodden ways, 49, 50, 61–2, 90
Simon Lee, 16, 21, 24, 60
Slumber did my spirit seal, A, 61–2

199

Strange fits of passion have I known, 61
Tables Turned, The, 47, 50–1, 57–9, 60
Thorn, The, 15, 16–17, 18–19, 20, 21, 22, 23, 24, 40–6, 55–6, 87, 107
Tintern Abbey, 64, 65, 69–73, 76, 77, 84, 86, 87, 89–92, 98–100, 101, 106–8, 110, 111, 112–14, 134
Two April Mornings, The, 60–1
We are seven, 47, 50, 51, 60
White Doe of Rylstone, The, 148, 151

Wordsworth: Prose Works

Prefaces, 10
   Advertisement of 1798, 40
   Preface 1800, 13, 36, 135, 180
   Note to 'The Thorn' 1800, 23–4, 40–2, 109, 2.5
   Preface 1802, 184–5
   Appendix to Preface 1802, 10, 12
   Preface 1815, 59, 4.17

Letters of Dorothy and William Wordsworth

Early Years 1787–1805, 88
Middle Years 1806–11, 72
Later Years 1835–9, 2.9
            1840–53, 1, 67
Dorothy Wordsworth's *Journal*, 149–50, 157

Coleridge: Poems

Ancyent Marinere, The, 24, 30, 124, 130, 148, 155–68, 182, 183, 184, 6.18
Christabel, 24, 30, 124, 130, 148–55, 156, 157, 161, 162, 167
Eolian Harp, The, 3, 130, 131 (Effusion XXI), 132–5, 141, 145, 181
Fears in Solitude, 130, 135–6, 139–41, 146, 147
Frost at Midnight, 68, 106, 130, 137–9, 141–2, 145
Kubla Khan, 124–30, 133, 137, 141
Melancholy, 139
Nightingale, The, 130, 143–4, 147
Osorio, 139
'Reflections on Having Left a Place of Retirement', 181
Remorse, 139
Sybilline Leaves, 131, 169
This Lime-Tree Bower My Prison, 68, 130, 134, 136–7, 138–9, 143–4, 145–6
Three Graves, The, 24

Coleridge: Prose Works

Biographia Literaria, 2, 8, 12, 13, 14, 41, 123–4, 148, 169, 182, 183
Letters, 123, 130, 4.4
Preface to Christabel (1816), 154, 156, 6.16

Index 2   Literary References

Arabian Nights, 128
Anderson, Robert, 2.9
Austen, Jane, 94
Ballads, 7–8, 24–5, 29–30, 162–7
'Barbara Allen', 7, 24, 56
Bible, 29, 67–8
Blair, Robert, 6–7 ('The Grave')
Blake, William, 8, 23, 1.5 (*Songs of Innocence* and *Songs of Experience*)
Bowles, William Lisle, 8–9, 181, 1.6, 1.7 (*Fourteen Sonnets*)
Burger, Gottfried, 7, 26 ('Leonore')
Burns, Robert, 5, 7
'Chevy, Chace', 7
Chatterton, Thomas, 7
'Children in the Wood', 56, 68
Coleridge, Henry Nelson, 148, 6.14
Coleridge, Sara (d.), 1.1
Collins, William, 5, 9, 86 ('The Passions'), 128, 133
Cowper, William, 5 (*The Task*)
Crabbe, George, 5, 6, 8 (*The Village*)
Dickens, Charles, 74
Godwin, William, 3
Goldsmith, Oliver, 5, 6, 8 (*The Deserted Village*)
'Good King Wenceslas', 24
Gothick literature, 6–7, 26, 67, 124, 126, 128–9, 148
Gray, Thomas, 9 ('Elegy'), 128, 133
Hakluyt, Richard, 157
Hartley, David, 123, 6.2
Hazlitt, William, 57, 3.6, 6.15
Horace, 6
Johnson, Samuel, 2.10 *Dictionary*
Keats, John, 150 'The Eve of St Agnes'
Lamb, Charles, 2, 93, 122
Macpherson, James ('Ossian'), 7
Milton, John, 3, 59 (*Paradise Lost*), 94, 112, 129, 5.10

Montagu, Lady Mary Wortley, 129
Monthly Magazine, 7, 182, 1.4, 2.7
Newton, Sir Isaac, 123 (*Opticks*), 126
'Ossian' (James Macpherson), 7
Parnell, Thomas, 6 ('A Nightpiece on Death')
Percy, Thomas, Bishop of Dromore, *The Reliques of Ancient English Poetry*, 7, 15, 24, 49, 56, 68, 142, 148
Pope, Alexander, 4 *Windsor-Forest*, 6 *The Rape of the Lock*, 10 'Essay on Criticism', 1.3 *Windsor-Forest*
Pre-Raphaelites, 151
Purchas his Pilgrimage (1613), 157
Quarterly Review, 6.14
Radcliffe, Ann, 6, 124 *The Mysteries of Udolpho*
Robinson, Henry Crabb, 2.12
Scott, Sir Walter, 7–8 1.4 (translation of 'Leonore')
Sea Journals, 156–7, 160
Shakespeare, William, 3, 59 *King Lear*
'Sir Cauline', 142
Southey, Robert, 1, 6, 122, 2.9
Spenser, Edmund, 3
Stanhope, Lady Hester, 129
Taylor, William of Norwich, 1.4, 2.7
Thomson, James, 4–5 *Seasons*, 9 *Seasons; Castle of Indolence*, 10, 11–12 *Seasons*
Walker, John, 2.10 *Walker's Rhyming Dictionary*
Walpole, Horace, 6 *The Castle of Otranto*
Watts, Isaac, 23 *Divine Hymns for Little Children*
Wordsworth, Mary, 1.1

Index 3 Language Topics

adjectives, 10, 10–11, 16–17, 31, 33, 42, 47–8, 49, 65, 66, 70, 72, 74–5, 76, 77, 80, 83, 84, 86, 89, 100–2, 129, 135, 136–8, 139, 146, 155, 160, 170, 171, 184

adjective complements, 18–19

adjective phrases, x, 49, 102

adverbs and adverbial adjuncts, x–xi, 19–20, 31, 33, 51, 52, 102, 170–1, 173–4

adverbial clauses, *see* clauses, adverbial

alliteration, 125, 127, 135, 149, 153, 165, 176

apposition, 18, 44–6, 48, 83, 98, 101, 140, 147

apostrophe, 21–2, 28, 47, 50, 51, 144, 174, 176–7

articles, 9, 11–12, 30, 49, 70–1, 79–80, 140, 146

associative language

sounds, 122–3, 124–8

words, 123–4, 128–9, 141–2, 144

back reference, 31–2

circumlocution, 37, 62, 76, 78, 81, 84, 86, 90, 100–3, 117, 118, 184

clauses x,

adverbial, 17, 49, 99, 173–4

co-ordinate, 17, 22–3, 25, 31–3, 48, 96, 99, 111, 145–6, 147, 149–50, 155, 165

correlative, 51

existential, 150

minor and verbless, 62–3, 144–5

non-finite, 19–20, 62, 112, 148–50, 175

participial, 80, 101, 149–50; past participle, 62, 98, 99, 101, 112; present participle, 65, 80, 84, 95, 98, 136, 149–50, 175; *to* infinitive, 19, 148–50

order of groups (SVCA), x, 17–18, 97, 116, 127, 142, 158

paratactic, 48–9, 150, 155

relative, 48, 49–51, 83–4, 94–5, 96, 99, 106–107, 112, 145, 150, 5.2

subordinate, 9, 17–18, 48, 49, 93, 94, 96, 99, 102, 110–11, 111, 113, 115, 145–6, 174–5

co-ordination, 18, 31, 32, 33, 177

see also clauses, co-ordinate

direct address, 21–2, 26, 28, 134, 143–4, 147, 158

eighteenth-century diction, 5, 8, 10–12, 65, 78, 81, 83, 85–6, 104, 106, 128, 129, 133–4, 140–1, 177

ellipsis and compression

diction, 77, 138

syntax, 49, 58, 59, 62, 96, 112, 115, 116–17

exclamation, 22, 27, 47, 50, 143, 144–5, 151, 152, 165

'expanded syntax', xi, 101–3, 173–4, 175

explanation of, 100–1

general and specific language

explanation of, 70

general, 9, 11–12, 66, 68–9, 70–6, 77, 78–9, 80–1, 81–2, 83, 84–5, 139–40, 144, 175, 4.8

specific, 9, 11, 66, 68, 69, 70–6, 77, 79, 82, 83, 84, 110, 4.8

grammatical metaphor, 53–63, 90–1, 172, 173–4

explanation of, 51–3

with inanimate subjects, 52, 58, 83, 90–1, 103, 108, 112, 114, 131, 137–8, 171

interpersonal expression, xi, 71, 98, 110, 113, 120

inversion, 18, 28, 29, 35, 44–5, 170, 171

see also thematic marking

202

language and registers
  archaic, 7, 28, 51, 78, 151–2, 156,
    166–7, 176
  ballad, 15, 20, 24–5, 26, 29–30, 43,
    48, 49, 56, 151, 156, 163–8
  biblical, 29, 67–8, 114
  cosmic, 16, 29, 43
  domestic and interior, 65, 66, 67–8,
    74–5, 76, 79–81, 81–3, 138,
    150–1, 153–4
  elevated and literary, *passim*
  of emotion 5, 16, 73, 85–9, 140,
    175–6
  everyday, *passim*
  exotic and oriental, 81, 124, 127,
    129, 160, 184
  formulaic, *see* proverbial
  Gothick, 6–7, 26, 27–8, 29–30, 67,
    128, 184
  historical, 151–2, 156
  legal, 68, 78, 81, 84
  magical and fairy, 124, 130, 133,
    141
  natural order, reversal of, 149–50,
    153, 159–60
  nature and rural, *passim*
  nautical and sea, 81, 156
  nautical journals, language of, 156,
    157, 159–61
  oriental, *see* exotic
  proverbial and formulaic, 21, 24–5,
    56, 164–5, 167
  Pre-Raphaelite, 150–1
  religious, 151–3, 155
  Romantic, 4–5, 26–8, 29–30, 67–8,
    79, 129, 156
  supernatural and sinister, 25,
    29–30, 128, 152–3, 155, 156,
    160–1, 161–2, 184
  urban, 73–5, 140
  war, 141
metaphor, 21, 42, 50, 51–63, 69, 75,
  77, 83, 90–1, 97, 103, 105, 106,
  130, 140, 171, 172, 176, 184
metre, 9, 15, 19, 23–4, 32, 35, 36–7,
  44–5, 45, 47, 93, 119, 154–5, 159,
  163, 184
modification
  nonmodification, 21, 31, 49, 72, 82,
    146
  postmodification, 19, 45, 48, 49–50,
    62, 65, 70, 80, 83, 84, 94, 96, 98,
    101, 138, 144, 172, 173

premodification, 10, 49, 70, 72, 80,
  83–4, 89, 100–1, 146, 170, 173
negatives and negative expression,
  61–3, 71, 89, 90, 96, 108–9, 110,
  112–13, 114, 118, 120–1, 125,
  134, 148–9, 152, 153–4, 172, 173
nominal groups, x, 10, 45, 46, 78, 80,
  83, 84, 100, 102, 145, 173, 175
  expansion of, 18–19, 45, 46, 48, 49,
    65, 70, 82, 84, 93–4, 94, 95, 96,
    98, 99, 100–3, 173
nouns, 16, 70, 86, 89, 91, 92
  abstract, 16, 33, 37, 47, 51, 54–5, 66,
    70–1, 77, 85–7, 107, 113
  compound, 77, 101–2, 138
  concrete, 16, 21, 33, 55, 69, 75
  plural, 11, 71, 72, 81, 84
  proper, 26, 27, 32, 74, 79, 124, 129
onomatopoeia, 52, 65–6, 172
passivity, expression of, 23, 38, 63, 66,
  100, 103, 103–8, 111, 114, 131–2,
  171
pathetic fallacy, 42
periphrasis, 11, 78
  see also circumlocution
personification, 11, 21, 50, 58, 91, 104,
  105–6, 130, 133, 177
prepositions, *passim*
  prepositional complement, 33, 45,
    55, 96, 117
  prepositional phrases, 100–3, 174–5
    and *passim*
  see also 'expanded syntax'
pronouns, 8–9, 23, 31, 32, 33, 71, 73,
  77, 98, 114, 115, 119–20, 143,
  144, 147, 171, 176
pronunciation, 32, 127, 2.10, 4.3, 6.4
reduplicative words, 26
register, 13–14, 55
repetition, *passim*
  clauses, 24, 25, 39–40, 43–4, 110,
    164, 175
  doublets, 25, 164, 176–7
  groups, 22, 25, 43, 110, 113, 130, 164
  sounds, 125–7, 149
  words, 16, 22, 25, 32, 38–9, 43, 56,
    110, 130, 135–9, 142, 149, 161,
    164, 2.5
rhyme, 10, 15, 20, 23, 25, 28, 36–7, 44,
  47, 127, 149, 154–5, 163
sentence structure, x–xi, 9, 15, 25, 38,
  93–4, 110, 114–21, 142–7, 156,
  172, 174–5, 184

sentence structure – *cont.*
  broken off sentences, 152, 156
  clause complexes, xi, 17, 25, 100,
    172, 175
  expansion, xi, 44
    clause, 48, 99–100; group, 18–19,
    48, 98–100, 100–3, 173–4
  presentative sentences, 145
  resumption, 95, 97–100, 106–7,
    110, 113–14, 144–5, 147, 175
  separation of group elements, 94–7,
    144, 170, 172, 173, 175
simile, 16–17, 21, 25, 30, 38–9, 41–2,
  47, 50, 56, 61, 75, 130, 133, 136,
  139, 140, 146–7, 155, 159, 160,
  161, 165, 172, 176
sounds, 65–6, 123–7, 133, 137, 149,
  174
  repetition of, 125–7, 149
specific, *see* General and specific
speech, representation of, 31–2, 34–5,
  37, 40–1, 44, 115–19, 143–4, 166
symbolism, 39, 55, 66, 78–9, 82–3,
  111, 116, 132, 133
tautology, 44, 45, 46, 2.5
tense, changes of, 20–1, 25, 33–4,
  165–6
  continuous, 20, 34, 171
thematic marking, 19–20, 29, 35, 38,
  100, 111–12, 115, 127, 158
  explanation of, 19

understatement, 40, 44, 62
verbs and verbal groups, x, 47, 52, 59,
  86, 89, 90, 91, 92, 113, 129–30,
  137, 171, 175–6
  auxiliary, 98, 166, 2.2
  cognitive, 176
  copula and lexically empty, x, 16,
    37, 38, 107, 130, 2.2
  to be, x, 16, 37, 90, 107, 171
  dynamic, 16, 37, 52, 75, 80, 83,
    89–90, 91, 107–8, 114, 171, 175–
    6, 2.2
  ellipted, 38, 49, 62, 144–5
  finite, 16, 38, 47–8
  of inert perception, 37, 91–2, 2.2
  intransitive, 107–8, 5.6, 5.7
  participles used adjectivally, 48, 75,
    89, 133, 171
  stative, 16, 38, 89, 89–90, 91, 92,
    113, 129–30, 171, 2.2
  transitive, 52, 107–8, 5.6, 5.7
  voice
    active, 92; passive, 38, 92, 103
vocabulary
  abstract, *passim*
  concrete, *passim*
  Latin and Romance origin, 16,
    47–8, 79, 88–9, 133, 170
  native stock, 16, 28, 37, 48, 51, 69,
    78, 79, 88, 89, 137